DECLUTTER YOUR MIND

A Life Changing Guide for You to Eliminate Stress, Remove Negative Thinking, Increase Happiness, and Overcome Anxiety

Alan O'Brien

© **Copyright 2017 – All rights reserved.**

In no way is it legal to reproduce, duplicate, or transmit any part of this document by either electronic means or in printed format. Recording of this publication is strictly prohibited, and any storage of this document is not allowed unless with written permission. All rights reserved.

Legal Notice:

This book is copyrighted protected. You cannot amend, distribute, sell, use, quote, or paraphrase any part of the content within this book without the consent of the author or copyright owner. Legal action will be pursed if this is breached.

Disclaimer Notice:

Please note the information contained within this document is for educational and entertainment purposes only. Every attempt has been made to provide accurate up to date and reliable, complete information. No warranties of any kind are expressed or implied. Readers acknowledge that the author is not engaging in the rendering of legal, financial, medical or professional advice.

By reading this document, the reader agrees that under no circumstances are we responsible for any losses, direct or indirect, which are incurred because of the use of information contained in this document, including, but not limited to, - errors, omissions, or inaccuracies.

TABLE OF CONTENTS

INTRODUCTION

CHAPTER 1: WE ARE WHAT WE THINK

How You Can Use Your Mind For You?

What is Clutter?

Decision Making – Making the Right Decision All the Time

How to tell you've made the right decisions?

Making a choice to Live Without Negativity

CHAPTER 2: WHY DECLUTTER YOUR MIND

CHAPTER 3: HOW MINDS GET CLUTTERED?

CHAPTER 4: TYPES OF MENTAL CLUTTER

CHAPTER 5: MINDFULNESS: FOCUSING ON PEACE

What Does It Mean to Be Mindful?

Buddhism

How to Achieve Mindfulness

Achieving Inner-Peace

Learning Relaxation

Posture

Meditation

After Meditation

Compassion

How to Live in the Present

CHAPTER 6: REMOVING BAD HABITS
How Bad Habits Influence Clutter Minds

Replacing Negative Thinking with Positive Thinking

Step-by-Step on Removing Bad Habits

CHAPTER 7: DEVELOPING UPLIFTING HABITS
How Good Habits Can Change Your Life?

Top 5 Best Habits for A Better You

CHAPTER 8: PROCRASTINATION
Letting Go of Procrastination and Fighting Against Distractions

Reasons for Procrastination

What Productive People Do

Methods to Stop Procrastinating

CHAPTER 9: WILLPOWER

CHAPTER 10: INVESTING IN YOURSELF
What Does It Mean to Invest in Yourself?

How to Achieve What You Want in Life

Minimalist Living

How to Become a Minimalist?

How to Feel Empowered In your Life

Changing Your Mentality

How to Find Your Passion?

- How to Become More Gracious?
- Stop Comparing Yourself with Others
- Removing Negativity
- Understanding Yourself on a Much Deeper Level
- How Can Failures and Setbacks Be a Good Thing?
- What are Your Values?
- Strengthening Your Work Ethic
- How to Improve Areas of Your Life

CONCLUSION

INTRODUCTION

How have you been lately? Do you feel worked up? Are you overwhelmed with many thoughts, worries, and concerns? Are you under constant stress? Deep down inside, are you happy with who you are and where you are? If you've answered 'yes' to any of the questions, let me tell you something. It is possible for you to be truly happy and for you to achieve a successful and fantastic life! Believe me when I say that we all want to live a simple and happy life. Don't think for a second that there is something wrong with you. A life that is free from negative thoughts and actions is a bliss anyone should afford. We can say that there are so many obstacles to living such a life, but the biggest obstacle of all resides in our own mind.

Human mind is capable of amazing achievements. Our mind and consciousness are the miracle that sets us apart from animals. Intelligence, rational ability, creativity, the ability to focus on a task or to project and imagine a future situation, in order to act on accordingly; all these abilities contribute to what the traditional definition of what a *complex and successful person* is.

As you might notice, all of this refer directly to the exterior world – to what we do, thanks to our mind, that benefits others & make us profit – money, power, influence – all of these assets come from the mind.

These are qualities that would impact not on the individual itself but on his image and actions that reflect the others. A more developed and trained mind paves the road to success. So, you might wonder, what is different about this particular guidebook?

In this book, you will discover how you can live life on your terms through a positive outlook and how to completely minimalize and organize your stream of thoughts to make your life a paradise, no matter your circumstance or context.

But before we proceed any further, I want to clarify with you that with this book, your life and your mind can totally be used beneficially for the achieving the best of YOU. Your mind is the strongest thing in this world. Thus, it's imperative to know how to control it and how to take care of it. However, this can only be achievable if you read the very content that this book contains and implant its teachings onto your life and others.

This book was written for anyone who believes in the sense of a more purposeful, productive, successful-bound life. And I honestly believe that through this book right here, that there will be a high and mighty chance for you to achieve that. And even after reading this book and whether you have any or no success on making your life better, at last, it will provide you with a different perspective and a more detailed plan on how to improve your life and mentality in any scenario or aspect.

Contrary to the general belief, when the actual focus is set on values like spirituality, serenity, simplicity and happiness, mind becomes the key obstacle. In an instant, our mind can transcend from being our best friend that helps us obtain money, recognition, social status and admiration from the exterior world into one of our worst enemies that lies within.

To put it simply: when our mind clutters, hell breaks loose.

As counterintuitive as it may seem to you at first glance, there is no direct connection between your mind and what you actually need to be happy. At the end of this experience, you will know exactly what I mean.

This is the core concept of this book. In a society that pushes our limits, wants us to be productive, respectful of the rules, obedient, our mind tends to act upon ourselves in order to signal that something is definitely off.

The compulsive thinking, defined as the inability to stop the stream of thoughts, manifests in virtually everyone. On the one hand, we have an amazingly complex paradigm of problems and conflict, on the other, we have an increasing input of info delivered by science that teaches us how to improve our mind. And yet we keep on failing whenever we try to be happy.

If you change perspective, you will soon start to observe what is the actual premises that make our mind clutter and continuously puts heavy weights on our soul.

It wouldn't be fair if I would have stopped here. If I take the responsibility to shout out about the issue, it is only natural to figure out some solution to it.

It's true that for some of you guys that read this intro, the actual shift in perspective could have happened already. Hence, you might want to skip directly to the chapters that underline and emphasize the DECLUTTERING – if you are an observant and self-aware person, you already know that your mind might work against you, so when you read about clutter, you don't feel surprised. On the contrary, you have a sense of confirmation, intriguing and comforting at the same time.

It happened to me too. This is one of the main reasons that I was fully motivated to write this book as a guide to de-cluttering and not as a critique of the actual state of human evolution. I felt something was totally off, as you do. While fighting to survive the intense stream of information, while trying to manage expectations and live up to standards, our inner self feels threatened. We feel this in our core.

This is it, guys. In times of trouble, mind tends to blame itself. It clutters and sends painful signals that slowly but surely put us down. Sadly, individuals that reach up to this point and don't have access to a shift in perspective engage in a fight with themselves that leaves them hanging to the edge of depression, anxiety, sadness, you name it. There is no winner, here, guys.

This is a fight you should not take alone. None of us should. This is the main reason behind my book.

Thank you for reading this book, I sincerely hope that you will enjoy it and that it'll help you along in life. With all that said, let's get started!

CHAPTER 1: WE ARE WHAT WE THINK

"We are what we think. All that we are arises with our thoughts. With our thought, we make the world."

Buddha

Maybe it's a new idea if I tell you that each one of your thoughts influences everything that surrounds you. Every second, every minute, and every day, your body is reacting to your thoughts, literally changing everything.

We are what we think. Your thought is merely projections of your reality. When you think of negative and evil thoughts, then those thoughts will only manifest in extra bad feelings and worsening experiences in the future. However, when you think of powerful and uplifting thought and declare positive affirmations, then it will render into a much more impactful life in the future. The whole world is all in your hands. But it begins by mastering your thoughts.

Every day, anybody can change their outcome of their life for the best or the worse, simply by changing how they perceive and think about situations. Positive thinkers might then reduce their stress levels, receive a higher salary, find a loving partner, and live a happy life just by changing the way they think about life and different situations. The way we think and how we focus on problems plays a role in how we live.

Now, it is easy to think of the many challenges we are facing in life. You can reflect on the pile of bills, being laid off, small salary, sick relatives, or not having a caring partner. We can all call them the struggles we face in life. But if you become more gracious and more confident about the situations, then your suffering will only repay you back into a greater amount of success and good feelings.

The hardest battle in your life is with yourself. It is when you fight with the person you are today and the person you want to be in the future. When you stop trying to find 'happiness,' then happiness will come to you by itself. Now, it is a big mistake to believe that you must work hard for happiness. But, happiness is already there, you were born with it! Happiness is merely the experience of your mind when fear is completely gone. Overall, being attentive about your thoughts, staying focus and positive might be challenging for some, but it is entirely possible!

The moment you change your mind is the moment you change your life!

How You Can Use Your Mind For You?

"What flows through your mind sculpts your brain. Thus, you can use your mind to change your brain for the better – which will benefit your whole being and every other person whose life you touch."

Rick Hanson

Right now, how hard will it be for you to be happy? What are some changes in your life or things that you can gain that will instantly make you happy? Money? Fame? Well, the most fortunate people to have ever walked on this planet often said that you would never find your true life's purpose when you look for these things. But they've often said that you'll find your happiness when you unlock your true character As I said earlier, it is easy for our minds to be plagued by the realities of this world or from the struggles you might be facing. But it can all change once you know how to use your mind to change the reality. It is easier than you can think.

You have the power to do things most powerful beyond what you can envision right now. In fact, you may be capable of things that you probably think are insane or impossible! Again, your mind is the strongest thing you have so you need to know how to harness it to its real potential and use your power of thoughts to shape the life you want.

Now, how your thoughts and how your mind scientifically can work for you is still a mystery today. Nobody fully understands how your thoughts can alter reality. Thus many people will often diminish these powers. It's almost like God; you can't get how God works, but you know that God is there. But the power of thought does exist, whether you are willing to accept it or not. If you don't, then you are only furthering yourself from your dreams and your full potential.

One example of the power of thought is the miracle of faith healing. Faith healing is a popular belief that quotes that anyone can become cured of any diseases, injuries, or setbacks through the power of prayer, divine intervention, or supernatural intervention. Though when you look towards prayer, it is primarily being used for your thoughts or meditation, which is directing outside from ourselves to the supernatural powers to achieve our desires. You can google search faith healing testimonies and find many real stories of people that have been miraculously cured o things such as cancers and other deadly impossible diseases. It often leads doctors to shock and science with no answers. It circles situations where there was no hope and medical science was far beyond their powers. But the fact is, the person held a belief so strong that they did not accept their fate or the medical report, but they intensely believed that they were the healthiest soul on this planet. Thus, making it real to everyone else.

So, how can one use their minds and thoughts to shape the outcomes of our life? Well, the answer is all of your belief. You must believe so strong and without the doubt and with all your heart and soul that you can and will fulfil your dreams and gain your desires. You must believe so deeply that it creates an intense level of intensity in your thinking so that your desires become only a burning obsession. You must be worthy to envision it and emotionalize it distinctly. The thought must consume you and become a part of you. You must believe at the level where you know that you can overcome any obstacle that may arise and that it is all true. That you will pay any price. You will give and do whatever it takes to achieve your goal. When you have a belief a strong like this, you invoke your superhuman powers of your mind to alter your reality. The world all relies on your feelings towards it!

These hardcore thoughts and feelings when focused in this manner will be recreated into your physical reality, what you were trying all so hard to desire. They are thousands of stories that claims this works. There are real-life examples and people who can confirm that whatever we want, we must firstly and genuinely believe that it is already there.

I know at first you might be reluctant to accept this truth. To the skeptics and doubters, I say that I hope that you are happy in your current circumstance. You must be happy. No matter how hard you fight or how much work you put forth without utilizing this principle of belief then you are limiting your life and your accomplishment. Just think about the many things you can do once you get past that limiting barrier. Our minds can only benefit us if we believe. The question comes to, will you believe?

WHAT IS CLUTTER?

So, know that you can conquer anything you want and get anything you want. Why is it hard for many? Well, it's because of clutter, mental clutter to be exact.

Mental confusion is merely thoughts and feelings and anxiety that is all clumped up together into your brain and is leading you into a state of self-sabotage, suffering, struggle, stress, and separation. Mental clutter is the thing that makes life hard and complicated. It is the stuff that puts us at odds with everyone else. We can't see them, but mental clutter will lurk around where peace and love don't. If we are cluttered, we are resisting the natural flow and ease of life. We are not allowing ourselves to reach our full potential or find our true life's meanings.

Like I said before if you hold an intensified belief of what you already have is there, then you will manifest it in your life. When you have mental clutter, it gets complicated; you will have too many thoughts making your mind heading in all sorts of directions. Maybe there is a voice inside your head saying that it is all meaningless. Then you have another voice in your head saying that it is everything to you and that you should never give up. Which one to follow? It will be hard.

If you are not experiencing openness, peace, and love, you have mental clutter. Most likely. It lives exclusively into your thought. And it only merely takes one negative thought or feeling to mislead you into a much bigger and destructive life. Now, there are eight common symptoms for mental clutter. When you notice only a small portion of one of these symptoms, then you have mental confusion, and you must take the initiative to get rid of it:

CONFUSION

Confusion is where you are often left misunderstood and uncertain about your thoughts and actions. It is where you are unclear about a something. It makes you feel powerless and impossible and often leave you with worry and fear.

NEGATIVE SELF-TALK

This negative self-talk is the voice going on in the back of your head. It is almost like your inner-monologue. It feels like a mental dialogue droning in the background; it keeps on telling you that you are a failure or that you can't do it. It is only merely insulting you every day.

When something bad happens, this voice is what makes you aware of it and makes you fearful of what will happen to you.

OBLIGATIONS

Obligations may or may not be entirely wrong. But, if you are feeling obliged to do something then you are experiencing mental clutter. It is where requirements influence you to the progression or an outcome of a situation. They are the demands and expectations that you put on yourself and onto others. They apply rules, boundaries, and limits onto your thoughts, feelings, and what you can do in life overall.

COLLECTIONS

Collections are the combination and grouping of objects. It is where you put labels on people and things. It is almost like a level of racism or pride, where you think that you are better than everyone else. It is where you want everybody to notice how hard you are working and to acknowledge your struggles. It can also be jealousy, where you envy someone because they have something you want.

COMPARISONS

Comparisons are the development of parallel or highest judgments. Comparing is the conscious thought where you take two things and putting them into war with one other for the purpose of choosing a preference, the best one. It feels like searching for bigger and better, like chasing and faster and stronger.

Comparing yourself or others are never good. Why? Because all of us are so singularly unique that we don't look the same, act the same, or think the same.

COMMITMENTS

Commitments are when you put your focus and all of your energy into a different cause or activity that is depriving you from your destiny or from who you are. We all do this, we all commit to attention and actions to all sorts of things, including family, work, wealth, dieting, relationships, meetings, appointments, projects, and more. It almost feels like you are merely piling up your days with all sorts of selections and responsibilities.

CONTROL

Control is where you put your power and thoughts to influence an individual behavior or the destined course of events. With control, we often seek power and to supervise the performance and behavior of life and other people to reap our desired outcome. It is where you feel like managing and manipulating events and circumstances in order to become comfortable and more confident with yourself.

Decision Making – Making the Right Decision All the Time

Decisions sometimes prove to be the hardest to make, especially when it's a choice between where you should be and where you really wanted to be

Decisions sometimes prove to be the hardest to make, especially when it's a choice between where you should be and where you wanted to be

In everyday life, we are often consumed with thousands of decisions. What to wear? What to eat? What to do? What to see? Who to talk to? Why should I do this? With all these consistent decisions, it makes us go back and forth and overanalyze situations until you drive yourself insane. Decision-making will often clutter our minds with all sorts of obligations, requirements, and duties that we must perform. And in many cases, with all these decisions and choices it prompts us to make lots of destructive decisions.

In this chapter, we will learn how you can always make the right decisions for the best of yourself. You will learn some tips that you must take to make the right choices, and that will reduce the amount of mental clutter and get you to feel more confident about yourself.

To solve difficult problems, you must make difficult decisions. These decisions must make you closer and more confident about not only your life but your future. Now, the only way to make the best decision is to weigh in your options and to go through them with logic and reason. You should also trust your heart and instincts while going over the options. Here are some tips to take to make the right decisions:

TRUST YOUR INSTINCTS

In many cases, your first impression reveals your correct decisions. This does not particularly mean you should rush yourself through and make the first choice in mind, but remember that seeking many opinions on something - whether it is a new place to move or a new job, it can confuse what you originally have wanted. To bypass the over complication and exaggeration of subjects, it is helpful to take a step back and to take a deep breath and to refocus on what you felt when you originally started to judge the best outcome of decisions.

HAVE TRUSTING FRIENDS TO HELP WITH YOUR DECISIONS

Instead of asking just anybody, from your mother to your mom's friend, to your waitress. Have a small group of trusted friends, relatives, or coworkers to act as your advisors. Make sure that these people know you well and can provide you with unbiased recommendations without pressuring you or getting way too involved in your life or the situation. It is always best to limit the number of people in this circle and to not have a large group.

DO NOT RUSH, TAKE YOUR TIME

In many cases, if you have been under pressure to decide on a decision it can make you more obliged to make a choice immediately before you have taken the necessary time to weigh in on your options. Most of the settlements you must make aren't made to decide quickly; it takes the time to pause and reflect on making the right choices. If you do rush yourself through the decision-making process, you might, later, regret it. If someone asks you for a new job, ask them to give you some time to study the situation and for a deadline for your response.

ASK QUESTIONS

Whatever the case that may be presented, you must ask yourself loads of additional questions to gather more information. Learning more and more about the many options laid out can not only assist you in making up your mind, but it will also enable you to feel more at ease with your choice. Now, when you are asking yourself questions, avoid asking yes or no questions. That's easy. Ask questions that can lead to a deeper and further discussion, to get a better understanding of it.

LEARN AS YOU GO

The more often you are faced with making tough decisions, the more confidence you must enable the ability to choose the right option. It does not happen overnight, but it will, slowly, as you become more comfortable and efficient in the decision-making process. It takes practice and can be turned into a decision-making formula.

Learn from your experiences, if you repeatedly make the same ole bad choices. Stop it! Choose the opposing one or don't make anything at all! Be open-minded and try new things to change the way you perceive the situation. Now, for many of us, it is not easy to feel completely ensuring in all of our decision-makings. We often contemplate over what might have been. Overall, to make the right choices, you must become more knowledgeable about the situation and to completely trust yourself.

How To Tell You've Made The Right Decisions?

Believe it or not, every decision you make not only affect us, but it affects the people around us. Even later ages are influenced by the choices we make. That is why it is imperative to make right decisions for the desirable outcome. Now, if you just decided and had second thoughts. Here are the things that tell, you've made the right decisions:

YOU LISTENED TO YOUR HEART

If you have a huge choice to make, whether it determines the best of your life or not. You must follow your heart. Now, when you did make the right thing. Did your gut tell you about the choice to make, or did a sudden sharp feeling told you about what must be done? Follow your heart and listen to instincts, gut reactions, and initiative guidance that can help you make choices that are in a position with your deepest values and concerns. But be cautious not to confuse your instincts with your emotions.

YOU WEIGHED THE POSSIBLE OUTCOMES

While listening to your gut and instincts are important sources of guidance, make sure that you also look at every decision rationally. Look at the pros and cons of each possible choice to figure out what is best for you, what makes the most sense for you. Balance out the emotional reactions by using logic and ensure that you have taken all the relevant factors of the decision into consideration.

YOU ARE CONFIDENT ABOUT THE DECISION

After you've made the decision, do you find yourself shameful or doubtful from these choices? Does your action potentially affect someone else in a negative way? If you are grappling with a decision between something you want and something you feel that you must do, take your time to contemplate how you will likely sense about yourself afterward - and whether the choice aligns you with the person you've wanted to change yourself to be.

YOU FOUND THE 'WHY.'

Have you gotten to the reason for why you might have been thinking about the situation? Why have you been cultivating about breaking up with him or her? Why have you been thinking about leaving your job to pursue your passions? Why have you been thinking about living your life in a healthier and positive fashion? You may tell yourself the countless of potential perks of such a decision without ever getting to the cause of your desire to leave a relationship or situation. Sometimes these details can fog our minds with negative self-talk and worry. That is why it's fundamentally empowering to ask yourself why you are making a choice in the first place. Why must you make this decision? Why is it very important? Looking at these questions will help find you the right thing and your real motivations.

AND MOST IMPORTANTLY, YOU CAN SLEEP

If you can't sleep, it can tell a lot about whether you've made the right decision. The moment after you've made that choice, do you feel tense or do you feel clogged up with anxiousness, racing thoughts when you talk or think about one of the options? Do you say to yourself that you should have gone back in time? Or, do you feel relaxed and confident about the future? Are you able to sleep regularly and with ease? By taking notice of these physical cues, it can help connect you more to numb feeling and instincts you may have about selecting an option.

Now, making active and right decisions will reduce the amount of mental cluttered and minimalize your life to a better you. And even if you do make the wrong decisions and are experiencing its effects. Use the power of your thoughts to overcome such setback and to guide your way to an answer.

MAKING A CHOICE TO LIVE WITHOUT NEGATIVITY

"Having a positive mental attitude is asking how something can be done rather than saying it can't be done."

Bo Bennett

Now after that section of making the right decision, I believe that we can all agree that one of the righteous decisions to make in our lives is to get rid of negative thoughts and feelings.

Negative thinking can have a high destructive impact on all aspects of our lives. It is never good. When you are drawn into the pattern of negative thinking, you are building a prison in your very own mind. It holds you as the prisoner.

Many people try many differentiated ways to break out of their negative thought patterns, only to beat themselves up and make it worse. If you are struggling with negative thinking, it is possible to turn things around and cultivate inner peace and happiness.

But first, is commitment! You must commit yourself and work very hard to remove negative thoughts and to create an intense level of happiness that will only render in the future.

Here are the four keys to break free of negativity for good:

RECOGNIZE YOUR NEGATIVE THINKING PATTERNS

Negative thought patterns are repetitive, unproductive thoughts. They do not have any real purpose, except to make you have negative emotions such as anger or despair.

Once you learn to recognize and identify with these negative thought patterns as they occur, you can start to have a decision about how to react.

MOVE AWAY FROM NEGATIVE THINKING

People who are swayed into their negative thoughts feel hopeless because they do not know what to do. It may seem like there are not enough answers to face your problems, you must plan for your future, and you must deal with the situations.

So how do you move through the course of days in a way that is thoughtful and genuine without getting engulfed into these cynical thoughts? Well, you watch your thoughts! To become free of negativity, you must be made more aware of your thoughts and what you put into your brain. Start to spend more attention to what is going on within your mind at any provided time.

Especially, put all your attention away from cynical thinking that may be arising. If you notice something that angers or worries you, do your best to solve it before it becomes a problem! Become an attentive observer of what goes on in your inner environment.

Each time your inner awareness is delivered to a negative thought pattern, it is only attacking you and persuading you to develop your mind in such. Go ahead and see if you can find these negative thoughts as soon as they arise before they gain too much force. If you cannot find these negative thoughts at first, then you do have another chance to become more aware of them and to respond with positive thoughts. For example, when a negative feeling comes into play, you can divert your attention to the thoughts of excitement that are being generated by such ideas.

BECOME MINDFUL

When you have negative thoughts, they circle two directions. They first circle the past; they remind you of your slips, obstacles, guilt and anything in your life that did not go the way you wished it has. The second is the constant worry of the future, it makes you fearful of what may or may not happen for yourself, or others.

We will learn this later in this book, but these constant worries can take a form of stress over whether you will achieve individual goals or anxiety about the security of your finances or relationships. Or maybe you worry about looking old. To get through these cynical thought patterns, your mind needs to cast its focus onto the past or future.

To become more fully awake and able to step out of this thinking pattern of worry, stress, and fear. You must redirect your attention and thoughts into here and now. Give your present moment your entire undivided attention.

CHOSE CONSTRUCTIVE THOUGHTS OVER DESTRUCTIVE THOUGHTS

So, now that you developed some inner awareness you can deliberately decide to change thinking, so that is constructive rather than destructive. Being positive is a choice. Being negative is a choice.

When you allow yourself to think constructively, you allow yourself to be happy when things are either going right and when things are going wrong. When you think constructively, you put problems into perspective and deal with them in a practical way.

Removing yourself from negativity will not happen right away. You must practice and practice to get better at it. The more you develop this awareness in your thought patterns, the more you can use your mind to cultivate happiness. To remove the mental clutter, you only need to take the initiative to remove them and to commit yourself further.

Chapter 2: Why Declutter Your Mind

One of the most prominent reasons you want to declutter your mind is because it already is playing a negative role in your life. You may be experiencing its effect right now and want to do something about it.

Most of the available resources we find online and in print when we look for help point out to dealing with the effects of the mind cluttering. Just like the traditional medicine nowadays, that uses treatment to deal with the symptoms mostly, and not with what is causing the symptoms. Self-help books easily tend to dismiss and overlook what is causing the symptoms – stress, anxiety, unhappiness and so on, and focus on the effects and how to treat it; if you feel stressed, try to work out more, if you feel tired, try to improve your diet, if you feel miserable, make new friends (...). I'm sure you got the point.

All these pieces of advice have a valid point. But in the end, if you look carefully at the bigger picture, you have to admit that something is missing. No matter how hard you try and sometimes succeed in tackling the symptoms that derive from a cluttered mind, sooner rather than later you will need to address the main issue you are facing. Your mind is slowly and steadily becoming your enemy – the cluttering creeps in, step by step, and only by realizing and reversing this process – the decluttering – you will be able to put an end to this spiral of unhappiness.

The benefits derived from dealing with the cause rather than the effects are huge.

Being efficient

It is hard not to notice that many of us who try to engage in dealing with the issues and problems we're facing in our day-to-day life have limited amounts of energy to spend. We all have to be productive, stay healthy, take care of others that rely on us for their well-being; at the same time, we have a job or are searching for a job, we are part of a family or a relationship, we have our dreams, desires, needs.

The obvious question arises. Is it worth fighting to deal with our own problems in such a way that we spend a great deal of time and resources? Does this struggle ends, eventually? Are we being efficient? I'm afraid the honest answer is not a positive one.

Vicious circle

As I mentioned before, most of the resources that are available for those who strive to achieve happiness in their lives are limited to dealing with the symptoms and not the cause. Moreover, at a more careful glance, we can observe a pattern that develops. How so?

When we approach an issue that is causing distress by tackling the issue in itself, not only we lose perspective, but we enter a merry-go-round that takes up a lot of effort and energy and gives us the illusion that we advance in exchange. After we deal with the social anxiety by making new friends, the next issue presents itself, for we've spent a lot of money and time and now we feel unsecure and stressed over our cost on day-to-day living. If we work more, to cover those new expenses, we end up stressed, tired, unable to maintain the relationships we just developed, and hence we get a new form of social anxiety and even worse, we feel disappointed, and we blame ourselves for that.

Stop. Take a step back. Unclutter your mind.

I've recently seen a funny pie-chart related to one's knowledge: a very small piece of pie represented what we know, a bigger one was representative for what we don't know, and the huge amount of the pie left was simply described as "What we don't know we don't know". Funny as it is, it actually has a point. It is virtually impossible to get hold of what you have no idea even exists. The same applies to the process of mind cluttering and the follow up – the decluttering.

We simply don't know it could be done with little effort. We have no idea that we stand close to the solution, for we are not assuming the correct obstacles. The following chapters will put things in perspective and deal with more detailed aspects of the core concept. For now, keep in mind that there is hardly anyone that can do this on its own. Knowledge is power, true, but at the same time, knowledge is shared and accumulated not as limited individuals, but as a collective mind that constantly improves.

If you read this book, half of the step back you needed to understand, at least, that there are some things you couldn't have discovered yourself, on your own, is done. The rest is even better. To put it bluntly, you already feel the answer to the "Why declutter your mind?" question. So let's engage in building up the whole perspective.

Chapter 3: How Minds Get Cluttered?

So how do our brains get cluttered? Well, everyone has either a tiny bit of clutter or lots of clutter accumulated in their mind. In this chapter, we will go over some of the reasons responsible for your brain getting cluttered with negative thoughts. We will tackle prevention of the cluttering, and we will have a look into one of the most common ways to break the clutter – live a simpler life.

As we already settled, the only best way to fight against and to declutter your mind is to be informed on why your brain is cluttered in the first place. In other words, one of the main reasons people have so much negative energy soaked inside their brains is because they lack knowledge on brain clutter. The majority of the population does not know what clutter is and explain it as something totally different, blaming context, the others, or themselves. While some of us might have heard of it, many are still relentless about it or have no idea such phenomena occurs.

The mechanism that clutters our mind is fueled by our uncertainty and social conventions. We live in a society that praises individualism, success, strength and determination. If at some point in our lives, we face obstacles in achieving those, some type of clutter begins to form. But is there a way to prevent it from happening in the first place?

There is good news and bad news. The good news is, being self-aware and having a more relaxed view on things can definitely prevent the starting of the cluttering process. The bad news is, staying positive and relaxed, without over stress about small and insignificant things is virtually impossible nowadays.

As we stated before, there are many similarities between the cluttering and a typical disease that affects our body, for example. As it's the case with conventional disease, in order to prevent, we have to take care of our bodies, to avoid exposing ourselves to bad influences – germs, viruses, bacteria –. It's safe to say that the mind follows the same pattern. In order to prevent clutter, we should not expose ourselves to bad habits, - stress, violent stimuli, overload of info -. Sounds pretty good, but is extremely hard.

There is no way we could pass through life without interacting with what the present times holds. Unless we choose from the start to isolate ourselves from all that is human and social, becoming monks or taking the ascetic road, it is obvious that we have to deal with the challenges and not run away from it.

Going even further with the comparison, a body that wants to prevent illness and disease cannot simply run away from pathogens, isolate from any possible harm.

That would achieve the opposite results: our immune system would not be formed, we would become weak and more exposed to getting sick. The same can be applied to our mind. It is never a solution to stay away, and even if some precautions should be taken, living life to the full is definitely the way to go about it. What if all of us choose to get away, to run from each other and isolate ourselves. Hard to imagine, isn't it?

We all know that when falling in love, for example, there is a great deal of risk that love will eventually cause suffering. But that never stopped anyone from searching love and exposing to the alter. We know the price, and we are happily ready to pay it. It is part of our existence, so we don't even question it.

The same applies to our mind and the risk of cluttering. Preventing the forming of such clutter is a definite possibility, but acting upon what our immense and complex and beautiful mind reveals is not debatable. We cannot just put half of our brain on pause. It wouldn't be fair; it wouldn't benefit anyone. So, we can only relay on staying on top of things, being informed and accessing the knowledge that could prevent the creeping in of clutter while at the same time enjoy the huge array of possibilities that derive from it.

- Simplifying Your Life to achieve happiness

One of the funniest things related to the act of simplifying our lives is that is a truly complex and complicated endeavor. Paradoxical, right? How come simplifying something can be complicated? Well, anyone that ever tried this knows exactly how hard and not at all simple it can be.

The new millennium brought into our lives a sense of time that is quickly running away from us, an infinite amount of knowledge that bombards us form a number of different sources, interactivity that could eventually get hold of our whole life, with the media and the internet and what derives from here and so on.

Even though it is hard to say these scientific and social achievements are harmful, for it wouldn't be fair, it is quite fair to take a step back and think again. Are those developments that we benefit off today directly connected to our level of happiness? Or, on the contrary, they tend to get in the way of us achieving serenity, joyfulness and blissfulness.

Simplifying our lives doesn't mean make it poor, or cutting ourselves form the delights of the modern society. Rather than that, it could mean getting to make a thorough selection and filtering of what actually enriches us. Once we get hold of that, by being honest with ourselves, we could start focusing on that and leaving all the detrimental side-activities outside of our horizon. Unfortunately, this is way easier said than done.

Chapter 4: Types of Mental Clutter

Mental clutter takes up plenty of space in your brain, making it harder to think through decisions and to enjoy life. If we let it, mental clutter will move and permanently soak inside our minds, developing a pattern that results in a full absorption of our mental energy and health. Our strong belief is that with just a little work, we can all find a way to cleanse our minds and move forward. But first, we must explore the types of mental clutter that exists, so that we become aware and able to spot them when they arise. The faster we spot some symptoms, the better:

These are the types of mental clutter that can be incredibly damaging over the long-term:

Worry

Worrying is never good. In fact, it's completely unproductive. And on some level, we believe that through worrying we can prevent certain events from unfolding and that we can control our future. However, it's up to us to act in such situations as the arise. The ability of our minds to project itself in the future is an amazing skill. Just like the possibility to recall the past and learn from it. However, there is a catch: when imagining future, we do so not by engaging in a rational analysis of facts and info, but we mix emotions, feelings, fear and uncertainty. Hence, whatever the future holds for us becomes an obstacle in our present moment.

Worry is the most popular forms of clutter as it blocks your mind from all sorts of gunk and leaves your brain less room for creativity or problem solving. As powerful a brain can be, it certainly cannot deal with the vast array of difficulties and problems that come up in our ordinary day-to-day road through life. It isn't fair to ask such things of ourselves, of our mind.

On the other hand, as great as it may seem at first glance, not worrying enough can also become a problem and make room for mind cluttering. Most of us feel that worrying is detrimental and thus they take refuge in all sorts of escaping methods. Either by overlooking the obstacles or by running away from issues and problems into destructive habits, dependencies, abuse of substances or chaotic behavior. We will talk extensively about these issues in a further chapter.

Regret

One of the most obvious forms of clutter is through regret. Now, you must know that there is not one single successful or happy person who has never decided that they've regretted one or more actions or events from their past. We all regret something, and we all make mistakes. It's part of what makes us human. However, it's up to us to decide whether we will let our mistakes define us or we will learn from them and move forward towards our well-being.

And by the way, we don't have to repeat our mistakes. We all heard that so many times. Don't repeat your mistakes, don't engage in actions that follow a destructive pattern, find the power to change when you've made a mistake. It is still very hard to do. It would mean we can both live our lives and also observe ourselves objectively and identify soft spots to work on. Even though it is hard or seems impossible most of the times, it is actually a very solid possibility, once we get hold of our mind and its tricks. If we acknowledge this fact, we can begin to see the past decisions or recollections that inspire us to feel regret as an opportunity to learn and change ourselves in positive ways. Regret is always unhelpful if it does not bring about learning or personal change. We could call it a waste. We can never change the past, but we can always change the future. We can make positive choices today, in order to ensure us against future regrettable decisions.

You know how they say there's something good in every bad thing. This is the case of regret; if we keep an open mind, regretting will teach us to finally accept past mistakes as an inevitable part of life and practice the important art of forgiveness.

Guilt

Life is always about moving forward., But guilt keeps us in the past, usually because we ponder about what we should or should not have done in certain situations. As you can imagine, our mind has the infinite ability to develop scenarios. It is a never-ending story. We all have been there. What if I would have said that, maybe I could have changed the outcome. The feeling of guilt is a strong motivator that keeps our mind focused on the past tense. Always reevaluating, always trying to absolve ourselves of any mistakes we've made. These mechanisms that our mind develop in order to keep us safe and comfortable can sooner or later have a big price. If not addressed wisely, after a while, guilt can soak into your brain, and it'll be almost impossible to move forward. It is not realistic to say that you'll forget what happened, but it is possible to release the past to live in the present.

Negative Self-talk

Our beliefs about ourselves, others, and the world as a whole can profoundly impact what we often say about others, our circumstances, and ourselves. Piece by piece and step by step, what we believe influences what we say and what we say defines how we behave. These belief systems we build for ourselves originate from many experiences we accumulate over our lifetime. One does not simply become a negative self-talker in a day; it takes years for such mentality to take place, but the reality is not very encouraging. So many of us misinterpret life circumstances, failures, other people behavior and we tend to take upon themselves.

But as we all know, negative self-talk is one of the worse mental clutters that can lower our self-esteem and hurt others even if it happens indirectly. When you boldly declare something insulting or not very complimenting about yourself, it creeps into your belief system and slowly but surely will manifest later in your life.

Attitude makes the difference! You might recall the famous words of one the most impressive president of the US, Winston Churchill that said: "Attitude is a small thing that makes a big difference". We couldn't agree more. If you go through life thinking that you are not good enough, you will never be good enough. It's that simple. Go through your life being self-aware, but try to figure out all the changes that you need to make. Not what others tell you, but what you feel about that. Write them all down. What are the life changes that you must make, because you feel it in your core, in your bones? That's the moment where you establish the foundational point to get you started.

Chapter 5: Mindfulness: Focusing on Peace

What do you think when you hear the word "mindfulness"? You probably might the ink of yoga, meditation, inner peace, or spiritual energy? Mindfulness is many different meanings to many different people, but overall mindfulness is all about being focusing fully on the present moment before us.

Becoming mindful will drastically enhance our everyday experiences, whether it is spending quality time with a loved one, eating food, studying for an exam, cleaning our body, or letting go of steam. In this chapter, you will learn all you need about mindfulness and how you can apply practical techniques to declutter your mind from negative energy and enhance many aspects of your life, such as:

- Relaxing your mind and relinquishing negative thoughts
- Reducing stress
- Reducing anxiety
- Overcoming depression
- Increasing your happiness
- Improving relationships

- Boosting productivity.

With that being said, let's get started

What Does It Mean to Be Mindful?

Really, what is being mindful? Well, mindfulness is a state of living in the present moment, without worrying about the future or being haunted by the past. When you are mindful, you become an observer of your own thoughts and emotions, without judging how you feel or how you are. Mindfulness is all about being awakened in life.

In all reality, anyone can become mindful; there are no barriers. Like I said at the beginning of the book, it is important to understand that you could change your perspective, you have control over your mindset. Everything you do and think affects your vision towards yourself, the ones around you and your environment.

Buddhism

To take a deeper perspective of becoming mindful, let me tell you about Buddhism in which mindfulness is very popular in the religion. Buddhism originated in the 5th century, in India with a man known as Buddha. Buddha is the first person to have ever reach nirvana and achieve a greater, more peaceful existence during his life. He believed that freedom or enlightenment in life came not from scholarly study, but by practicing meditation and mindfulness.

Buddhism is a religion of inspiration. It is about exploring who you are in relation to the world around you. IT is not self-worship either. It is an exploration, and you will see from the story of the roots of Buddhism that someone already did all the legwork for you. All you need to do now is to follow that lead, and you will indeed realize your ambitions to become happy and to live a peaceful, enlightened life.

One day when Buddha saw suffering, he was extremely unhappy and unsettled. He felt so strongly so about it that he wanted to find out what the root cause of this suffering was. People looked away from those who were ill. People disregarded death and refused to accept that death I merely a passage that happens in life. What Buddha saw was that if people are not certain standing in health or were a little different from the norm, they were either ignored or became less than other were seen to be. He found this very disturbing and sought to find out why people suffer and what could be done to stop this suffering. He had already learned the art of meditation but had not yet learned of its great significance since his world had been so protected from the realities of life.

What we found changed the way that people approach life even in the day. In answer to hi question of why suffering exist, he found that much suffering caused to mankind was caused by mankind and by putting together the rules that make up the basis of Buddhism, he could diminish suffering and enable people to change the e-course of their lives by changing their actions, their attitudes, and their prejudices.

The Eightfold Path was born because of his meditation and when he saw how clearly the thought came, constructing the Eight-Fold Path became his life's work as the First Buddha.

You may wonder what the Eight-Fold Path is all about and your natural curiosity may be asking how people can make they're live devoid of too much suffering simply by changing their actions. However, what he found was so positive that it has lasted and the Buddhist monks of today are simply following in his footsteps hoping, through meditation, to reach that Nirvana or understand what Buddha was trying to reach

The Eight-Fold Path includes the following elements:

- Perfect Vision- Seeing things in a clean manner based on understanding rather than guesswork
- Right attitude – or the ability to let go of the negative and learn compassion
- Right speech – saying the right thing, speaking afterthought rather than without it.

- Right action – doing what is morally right.
- Right livelihood – in other words taking no advantage of people, moral work.
- Right effort – putting in the effort that is required
- Right mindfulness – being thoroughly aware
- Right concentration – this is more than effort. It is discipline.

Buddha believed that those who reached true nirvana would leave behind the physical world for good, the soul will not reincarnate and return to the earth. It was more than just freedom from suffering. Buddha believed in a pure il be where one conducts altruistic acts, versus those from elf-benefit.

There are Four Noble Truths that are part of the Buddha's teachings. These Noble Truths are in a simplified version:

1. Suffering do not exist
2. Suffering occurs only because of one's desires.
3. Suffering will end when the desired ends
4. Freedom from suffering require the practice of the eightfold path

Each of these noble truths will be discussed in further detail. For now, you need to know they are the core teachings to reach a peaceful, mindful way of life.

How to Achieve Mindfulness

For one to achieve mindfulness, practice and patience are necessary. But before we work on the methods to achieve mindfulness, we must direct our perspective to the element that causes us not to be naturally mindful. Meaning you must understand suffering.

With the understanding of suffering, you can stop being manipulated by your own emotions; we allow ourselves to resolve our inner torments and open space for personal growth. To become mindful, we must first become compassionate towards ourselves.

To be compassionate towards the self is about accepting your mistakes, understanding why you are the way you are, understanding that no one is perfect and that include you, acting with kids towards your imperfections.

Achieving Inner-Peace

A part of achieving inner peace is about meditation practices. There are several meditation styles that you will learn about and can adopt to work your way towards inner peace. The ten concepts listed here are things you can do at your own pace to attempt to reach inner peace.

Forgiveness

Forgiveness is a pathway to inner peace. How can you see another person and their thought, or even be more altruistic if all you can feel is ire? Forgiveness is not about accepting another person's immortality Do not get the two confused. Forgiveness is measured of letting your negative emotions go and ensuring that you do not peel vengeance, a need for revenge. It does not can you accept who at another s done, but that you reach a state that you can be happy again. Letting in negative emotions bring in bad karma. It is far better to forgive, accept that you cannot change the past, and allow another' bad karma to take care of them.

(Karma is a sum of action a person has conducted in previous and current existences. It is the term that describes the fate of th e future existences. For instance, let us say that someone consistently behaves unethically. Life after life, they end up in jail because of mistakes they make. Until this person is reborn and learns from their past mistakes, they are not going to be able to solve their own negative fate. For you to gain good karma, to determine a better fate in this life or the next, you need to be willing to forgive and let go. When you forgive, your soul will be at peace, your mind will relax, and you can focus on more important things. You can also start helping others.

Concentration

Gain better concentration through meditation, only as a pathway to inner peace. The more you can concentrate and focus on all tasks in your life, the easier it will be to feel comfortable and happy within your own skin. If you cannot concentrate on the task at hand, where your mind is thinking a million thoughts at once, then you are going to suffer. Concentration also allows you to stay on task and meet deadlines in personal and professional settings. If you notice that you are missing deadlines at work, and you often flit from one thought to the next, rather than the task at hand, take the time to meditate.

Through meditation, as well as other steps in achieving inner peace, you will only find a way to get back on target and take control of your life.

Music is another way to help with meditation, as well as finding a sense of calm. Have you ever heard someone say this music truly touches my soul? IT is because they are hearing the music chords and/or words more deeply. Yes, you can hear the background music, but the important part about listening to music is to relax the soul, it is not concentrating on the music in detail. They are listening instead to the rhythm of their heart. The rhythm that slows down to relax when the music touches their soul. The music used to calm your inner self can differ from day to day. Christmas music might be great because of the happy feelings it provides, but at other times, you may need lyric, free music like ocean and nature sounds. If you want to speed up your work, you might choose something fast paced that helps your mind relax, and your soul connect. It all depends on your mood and the type of inner peace required.

Learning Relaxation

You may not know this, but the way that you breathe has a lot to do with how much you suffer from stress. If you breathe in too much oxygen, you can become hyper active and very nervous indeed as a result of this over oxygenation. If you're breathing shallow, you are not allowing your brain to have sufficient oxygen. The way that you breathe really does make a difference in achieving a full state of mindfulness because it helps you to achieve meditation. People think that meditation is simply matter of sitting doing nothing, but it is much more than that. It is all about getting closer to Nirvana or that place where you find an answer to all of life's questions. It also helps you to lower your blood pressure, slow down your heart and give your body and mind a chance to get together and to sharpen all your senses

The way that you breathe also helps you to be able to meditate and relax. You also need to be able to relax and enjoy life more. If you are one who works very hard you might find relaxing to be hard. That's why practicing relaxation techniques is important as well as being able to breathe in the best way possible.

Posture

Posture is important; the chance that you take when you do meditation is for a purpose. In the human body, there are energy points that are known as chakras. Chakra is in a straight line from the top of your head right down to the tailbone of ah man being. If you slouch when you sit, you are likely to have problems allowing energy through the chakra that is being pushed out of position by your bad posture. Similarly, if you experience pains around the shoulder and neck area when you are stressed, it is because the chakras in the neck are blocked, and energy cannot pass through it. Thus, you need to learn the significance of posture to the response your body gives you to live in general.

The standard sitting position for meditation is sitting on a yoga mat on the floor with your legs outward and your knees bent. Your ankles are then crossed. Of course, more advanced positions exist, but there are not there for beginners. They are for people who have learned over many years how to position their feet and legs into the full lotus position. You won't be able to do this. You can also meditate sitting on a hard chair if your mobility is limited, but the most important point is that your body is centered. Thus, sit on a cushion on the floor, bend your knees and cross your ankles. Place your hands on rested on the other with your palms facing upward. Now, rock your body until you feel that it is in the right position. The good place is the comfortable position you know you can stay in without toppling or moving during your meditation. You will not know that your back is completely straight and that's part of posture that is critical indeed.

Posture in general

If you find that your shoulders slouch in life, you need to respect that they need to be straight. Your legs should not cross as this can restrict your blood flow.

Your feet should be flat on the ground when you are sitting on a chair. Many people take little notice of posture, but if you were to watch a monk sitting meditating, you would notice that there is a straightness to his back, that his head may be slightly bowed and that his hand will most certainly not be fiddling around, but will be placed one on top of the other. They put the strongest hand to the bottom to support their weak hand, which means that if you are right-handed, your right hand will be considered as the most powerful side.

The reason posture makes such a difference is that many of the ailment that you suffer from can because of a misalignment of the spine. If you add to that fact that you are now trying to eat in a mindful way, you are improving the way that your body responds to the life that you impose upon it, and many exercises can help you to respect your posture. If you find that there is a local yoga class, join in. It isn't something trendy. In fact, you are likely to meet like-minded people who are trying to improve their mobility and their life by taking yoga classes.

Many of the exercises that are used in yoga help you to increase your mobility, but they also work with the way in which you breathe, and that's vital to success with yoga.

Think of the chakras as energy points that go from the top of your head right down the spine to the base of the spine. There is one chakra that is slightly different in that is located in the heart region, but if you have started to exercise gentleness with the people around you, you have already helped this chakra to stay open to energy flow. Angry people tend to have this heart chakra closed, which is another reason to avoid anger and negative feelings

Stretch regularly. Keep your spine upright when you are sitting and take regular walks as this helps mobility. It also helps you to regain energy that may have been lost over the course of your life. Slouching in front of the TV isn't helping you much, and if you can devote some of the time to meditation, you will find that you feel a lot better about the energy that it gives you. You must remember that when you are lethargic that energy creates energy. Thus, walking and doing the kind of sport that you consider within your capability will help you to keep chakras open. Swimming is great low impact exercise and can help your posture as well.

Your position is crucial. If you allow bad habit to develop, you block your energy center and will suffer because of this. One of the thing that Buddha noticed was that many were suffering from their physical ailment and his ideas were put into use bearing in mind that not everyone is in tip-top condition. He wanted to stop suffering for all mankind, and that include those who are infirm. Thus, you can improve your health and diminish suffering by taking this chapter very seriously.

MEDITATION

Meditation is part and parcel of the mindfulness and decluttering of your mind. It is more than thinking about nothing. People who have never tried meditation often have the wrong impression of what it is all about. IT is a quieting of the mind, allowing the subconscious mind to work away in the background unimpeded by thought from the conscious mind. The problem is that in our day-to-day lives, we suffer from the overload of stimuli. We watch TV; we travel with cars, we look into computer screens, and there are so many people differing views in our lives that we are left with thought processes which are potentially holding us back from being who we are capable of being. Meditation helps to put that back into balance, but it does much more than that. It allows you think clearly, to be more productive and to have a closer connection with your own sense of spirituality. It

Preparation for meditation. Preparing form meditation means to make pace where you will meditate a part of your daily routine. Unless you meditate daily, you won't get the best out of meditation. It takes consistent practice, and it takes discipline and that' something that is baldy lacking in today's world. Thus, this space that you create helps you to keep your promise to yourself that you will indeed meditate.

IN Buddhist temples, you will find many flowers, statues, and paintings as a source of inspiration from which people are able to glean all that they need in order to meditate and to gain what they can from meditation.

Thus, you may want to decorate that part of your home that you use for meditation. Perhaps that there are little statutes that will make the area more inspirational. You might also want incense sticks and candles.

As you get more experienced in meditation, you will spend more time meditating through choice. However, since this is only the start of your experience, expect to spend between 20 minute and three-quarters of an hour on daily meditation. You will need a place in your home where the air is fresh and where the ambiance is the perfect for a relaxation session. Thus, it's best to choose somewhere that isn't too hot, or that isn't too cold.

As you get ore experienced with meditation, you will be able to use inspirational places to meditate such as beaches at sunsets or sunrises, or unusual places that you love which bring you close to nature. However, in the initial stages, these will bring too many distractions, so your meditation space in your home should be somewhere you can relax and away from distractions.

You might have a special pillow or an outfit you will like to use for meditation, though it may cause distraction later on.

You also need to talk with anyone that you are living in your life not to bother you while you meditate. This should be a quiet time with no interruptions at all, and if that means that family turns down the TV or music being played in the bedrooms, then they should respect that you need this time. It's only a short length of time and insisting upon it being a time when you will not be disturbed by their noise is not unreasonable.

 Preparing for mediation is imperative. IF you start to meditate before having preparation, the chances are that you will be disturbed and that will be enter into a pointless meditation session. If you are going to the trouble of meditating on a daily basis, you need people to respect that, and you also need to have the space prepared in advance so that your chance of successful meditations is assured. You will also need to choose a time of day when you have not just eaten or when you can relax and switch off.

During meditation, turn off your cell phone. If you find that clocks distract you, place them in a different room. Some people who meditate enjoy the ticking of a clock and use it to count to. However, others find that it I very distracting. You need to prepare changes in your environment to suit your own style of meditation and your own sensibility.

Meditation

To meditate, you need to be seated in the right position. If you have limited mobility, you can use a hard wooden chair and place your feet firmly flat on the ground. Your back must be straight. If you do not have mobility problems, you should sit either on a cushion or a stool especially made for meditation and bend your knees. Your ankles should be crossed. Your hands should be placed on your lap with your strongest hand supporting the others, palms upward.

Now sway a little until you find that perfect position in which you are comfortable it I win in the first stage of meditation that you do not miss out the swaying movement because otherwise, you may find half way through meditation that you are feeling uncomfortable.

That is called grounding and just means making sure that your body is correctly seated and that you can stay comfortable during meditation.

Breathing

Breathe through your nose and feel the air going inside your body. Instead of thinking of air as oxygen, think of air as your number one source of energy. Hold the breath for a moment, and then let the breaths out. Keep doing this until you establish the correct rhythm where your breathing creates that pivot in the upper abdomen. When you have regular breathing to a rhythm, you will be able to start your meditation. Close your eyes.

1. Breathe in through the nostrils – think of nothing but the breath for the count of seven.
2. Hold the breath inside of you for the count of 5
3. Breathe out to the count of eight
4. Count the number one

All the time while you are doing this, you are thinking of nothing except the exercising of meditation. You will have thoughts creeping into your mind. That's normal when you are not experienced at meditation. When this happens, acknowledge the thought and then let go of it, going back to the exercise shown above. You continue to breathe in this way and each time you complete a cycle you use the number two, three, four, five, six, etc. until you reach to teen. You will inevitably go back to the number one several times. That's normal, and most people have to do this.

I will set the first session of 35 minutes, but not longer than that. It is better that you have shorter successful sessions than trying to force yourself to stay in meditation for longer when you are not experienced.

All of the time that you are breathing in the way shown, you concentrate only on the breathing and the counting. Nothing else should interrupt your thoughts.

What you'll gain from mediation?

You gain the ability to control your thought patterns so that the subconscious can experience being at one with your conscious mind. Since your conscious and is almost silent or busy with the task of breathing and counting, your thoughts are not getting in the way of being able to reach inside of yourself. When you're have been doing meditation for a while, you will find it will improve your outlook on life, it will make you feel energized, and it will shape the way that you thin in ways that perhaps you will never expect.

What is the prize? What is the goal? The goal for all of your real action is that you can feel actions from within. If you are mean minded and critical of other, you cannot find the same kind of inner peace that those who feel compassionate Thus you stem your chances of happiness. Practicing compassion makes you a better person from inside out, and you will find that life chance for the better once you embrace it and make it a part of who you are. Contrary feelings towards others do nothing to feed your soul. Positivity towards others helps to show you your strengths. When you make mistakes, use these steppingstones to move forward – letting go of negative patterns of behavior or self-doubt. Negative feelings will stem your growth – whereas compassion will help you to grow into a happier human being.

AFTER MEDITATION

It is important that you respect your body. Your heartbeat will be slower, and your blood pressure will be low when you have finished your meditation sessions. Thus, don't get up and run back to your busy life. Instead of doing that, go over your session in your mind and decide what you can do better next time, or that you are simply going through a learning process. This is important and allows you a little extra time while your heartbeat comes back to normal, and your blood pressure normalizes. It will also mean that the next time you decide to meditate, you will be able to use those thoughts to improve the experience even more. Once you have tried meditation, there are various other types of meditations that you can work such as chant meditation or mindfulness meditation, though mastering the basics will help you become accustomed to the discipline involved.

COMPASSION

What is the prize? What is the goal? The goal for all of your real enterprise is that you can feel actions from within. If you are mean minded and critical of others, you cannot find the same kind of inner peace that those who are compassionate. Thus you grow your chances of happiness. Practicing compassion makes you a better person from inside out, and you will soon find that life changes for the better once you embrace it and make it a part of who you are. Contradictory feelings towards others do nothing to feed your soul. Positivity towards others help a great deal revealing your own strengths. When you make mistakes, use these as stepping stones to move forward – letting go of negative patterns of behavior or self-doubt. Negative feelings will never act like a stem for your growth – whereas compassion will help you to grow into a happier human being.

HOW TO LIVE IN THE PRESENT

Living in the moment is not always easy. Sometimes our thoughts are overwhelmed by regrets about past events or anxiety about the future, which can make it hard to enjoy the present. If you are having a hard time living in the moment, there are some simple strategies that may help. There are little things that you can do throughout your day, such as creating a mindfulness cue, learning to meditate, and performing random acts of kindness. Keep reading to learn more about how to live in the moment.

1. Do one thing at a time.

Single-task, don't multi-task. When you're pouring water, just pour water. When you're eating, just eat. When you're bathing, just bathe. Don't try to knock off a few tasks while eating or bathing or driving. Zen proverb: "When walking, walk. When eating, eat."

2. Do it slowly and deliberately.

You can do one task at a time, but also rush that task. Instead, take your time, and move slowly. Make your actions deliberate, not rushed and random. It takes practice, but it helps you focus on the task.

3. Do less.

If you do less, you can do those things more slowly, more completely and with more concentration. If you fill your day with tasks, you will be rushing from one thing to the next without stopping to think about what you do. But you're busy, and you can't possibly do less, right? You can. I've done it, and so have many busy people. It's a matter of figuring out what's important, and letting go of what's not.

5. Put space between things

Related to the "Do less" rule, but it's a way of managing your schedule so that you always have time to complete each task. Don't schedule things close together -- instead, leave room between things on your schedule. That gives you a more relaxed schedule and leaves space in case one task takes longer than you planned.

Redirect your mind when it wanders. It is normal for your mind to wander, but in order to live in the moment; you need to keep your mind focused on the present. When you notice that your mind is wandering, use gentle redirection to focus on the present again. Acknowledge that your mind is wandering without judging yourself for doing so.

Don't get upset at yourself if your mind wanders. It is normal for your mind to wander sometimes. Just accept that you took a little mental vacation and return your focus to the present.

Live in the present life.

Most of us tend to relive the past, and most of us are always considering the future rather than focusing on the existing time. Living in the present is showing us that we are aware of what's happening on right here and right now. When we live in the present, you demonstrate that you are living where life is taking place.

When we choose to live in the past or future it steals ourselves from the enjoyments of today; tomorrow is never promised, and we cannot travel back to the past. The only significant moment in your life will be the present moment.

Focus on the moment you are in right now. One incredible way for you to let go of the past and for you to put your worries of the future to a stop is to put your energy into right now. If you go to work with the same ole working mindset, then you are not living in the present, you are residing in the past. Always look at things like it's the first time you are experiencing it.

Life is too short for you to be spending all your time caught up in depression, you are going to miss many of the joys and surprises that life gets to offer. An unenthusiastic person might not even know that there are good wonders right in front of them, rather they will choose to focus on the negative and not on the positive.

Sit yourself down and think about the many times that life has destroyed a relationship or have caused you to miss a happy day of your life. That's time that you will never get back in life. Start to live your day as if it is your last, what will you do differently? If you only had 24 hours left in this world, will you use that time to complain and to criticize about yourself and others, or will you spend that time doing the things that you have always wanted to do and to give an insane amount of love to everybody you meet? To start living your day to the fullest, just ask yourself something. What do you want in life? What are your dreams that you want to achieve in life? There are no obstacles, there is only the will take you there.

Have clear communication

One of the most important elements in productivity and working with others is communication. Having excellent communication that is transparent, open, honest and respectful will provide others to be themselves and prevent any negative attitudes and anger in the future. You should encourage others to ask questions and to listen to one another. This helps build better teams and stronger loving relationships.

Have respect for yourself and others

Respect should always be taken accounted for to the utmost. It's important for you to understand and to respect your peers and your superiors. When you are with your coworkers, and you know the diversified skills and personalities that consist of this company, then you will be able to accomplish anything in life. Each person needs to contribute their strengths to grow in life.

Be open-minded and keen to new ideas.

Open-mindedness is one of the most sought-ought traits for employees. Being open-minded means that you have a willingness to listen to other ideas and opinions and consider the possibility taught you are wrong or may change your perspective. This can be an outstanding quality in the workplace.

It is critical to job success. Personalities want to know that you have a willingness to learn new things and consider alternative approaches to problem-solving. Without this spirit of listening and cooperation, it will be hard for you to complete projects and to optimize on quality.

Have a good reputation

When you are in the workplace, you want to establish a good reputation. Taking up your professional reputation, you need more than just a good everyday performance. Changing the way your coworkers and employers see you may be difficult, but it is entirely possible. To gain a remarkable reputation at work, you must get individuals to notice a brand-new behavior about yourself. You must keep up a positive attitude when all in doubts and remain consistent in your noble profession for the best for everybody.

Maintain your health.

Wellness is important if you want to keep up in living a happy and fulfilling life. Science has linked to our mental and physical health to play a factor in our work performance. Eating well is the best way to control your health. Look at your portion size when preparing meals and eat plenty of fresh fruits and veggies.

As well with that, exercise daily. Exercise has numerous of health benefits and can make you instantly better about yourself when you go to work. In fact, it has been proven that if you do cardio for 20 minutes in the morning, you will feel productive and confident by the end of the day.

Always continue to learn.

Obviously, learning is very importance. Knowledge is power. Learning creates positive energy through inspiration and new possible. Learning will allow you to keep your minds active and to take on more challenging duties in the future as well of new opportunities and friendships to come.

The more you know, the more you will be able to control the events that unfold in your life. You will he the power to achieve many things. You gain valuable information that can affect outcomes of stressful situations. Just being prone to learning something every day., such as reading articles online, dedicating yourself one hour every day to read up on your self-improvement, and ask advice from other people.

Surround yourself with enthusiastic people.

To improve the circumstances in your life and to make your life always exciting you must only surround yourself with passionate and inspiring people. Believe me when I say that this is the most important aspect in always remaining enthusiastic at work. The power of enthusiasm is so strong that it will affect others around you and whenever you feel down in the dumps, and then you can rely on others to lift you up.

To surround yourself with rich people, you must become optimistic as this gives you a brighter identification for some. Like attracts like. When you are in a positive mindset, then others will be attracted to you. Surround yourself with others who believe in your dreams and help motivate you during the struggles. Even if you do not have that inspiring person at work to look up to you can listen to audio found online of enthusiastic people such as Tony Robbins online. Enthusiasm is contagious so use that to benefit yourself and others.

Have patience.

It takes patience to achieve something worth reaching. Growth and learning new skills take time, so do not rush yourself through it. Moving on through resentment doesn't take a day; it takes plenty of steps and a long time just to feel free and healed. So just know that working in perfect harmony will take time.

Today, I want you to take on one step at a time. Let the trouble from the past move on and allow new experiences to come. Give yourself the needed time and permission to explore and to heal, and then you'll achieve perfect harmony at work.

All this useful advice and implementing these thoughts inside your mind can help bring peace in your work life and your private life. We need to remember that we are the deliberate creators of our life and we can choose whether we want to have an exciting life or a dull one. The choice is always yours.

Chapter 6: Removing Bad Habits

In life, we all have bad habits that we need to get rid of? Such habits are not helping us reaching our full potential and live the life we always wanted to live. Some habits are destructive and hurt others in subtle ways.

In this chapter, we will look at what you can do to replace your bad habits. Let's look at these methods.

How Bad Habits Influence Clutter Minds

As we all know, bad habits are never too good to have in our life. Bad habits can clutter our brain and make us think irrationally at every given second. Here is a list of only a minor of bad habits that most of us may have:

- Snacking when not hungry
- Smoking to
- Worry
- Angry at certain situations
- Drug use
- Watching too much television
- Swearing
- Interrupting

- Lying
- Overspending
- Procrastination

As the list mention above, we can all immediately list the reasons on why such habits are bad for us. Habits are the things that you do repeatedly often regularly, and even unconsciously.

If you look at the habits of highly effective people, they don't have many insecurities or any bad habits lurking around. Those who progress in life have kept learning new things rather than resisting the change to replace old habits. They key is identifying the habits that are useful and eliminating the habits that are not.

REPLACING NEGATIVE THINKING WITH POSITIVE THINKING

You will find that it is very easy to get caught in the snare of 'negative thinking' when it comes to succumbing to that bad habit, you so clearly wish to steer away from. You need to understand that there will be times when you will be severely tested by the thoughts that seem only to cause havoc in your mind; thoughts that it will only serve to alienate you from those good habits you are out to perform the process of validating those bad habits you already have.

For instance, you might be thinking that it is far better to be lazy rather than going to the gym. In which case, you need to make sure you immediately stop and eliminate those thoughts and replace them with positive thoughts. For example, instead of thinking that it's much better to be lazy say to yourself that you are not going to sit there and feel sorry for yourself. You are going to the gym right now to make a difference about the way you feel.

You will see just how powerful a thought like this can be when it comes to making sure that you are well on the track to replacing your bad habit with a good one that will surely hold you in a good stead!

The only thing you need to understand is that the only way you can lead a richer, more productive and fulfilling life is by making sure that you make an effort to incorporate good habits into your life. The thing that holds most people back is the fear that they cannot sustain the kind of willpower that is needed to maintain a good habit, for too long. That is what needs to change; one has to understand that you only need a little bit of willpower in the beginning, when you are in the process of forming a new habit.

In the end, you will find that you are repeating those habits unconsciously and that there is on absolutely 'no willpower' required by you anymore. All it takes is a little effort in areas like health and fitness, productivity, and even personal development to ensure that you are well on the path to a 'better life' through the deployment of good habits that are really engineered to change your life for the better.

In Chapter 7, you will learn some uplifting habits that can only benefit you in life and in the future.

STEP-BY-STEP ON REMOVING BAD HABITS

Removing bad habits in your life can be rather simple depending on how long you have carried on the certain habit. If you carried on a habit for years, then it will be much harder to break the habit than someone who has recently start carrying the habit:

1. To start you want to acknowledge that you have a bad habit and make a commitment to yourself in letting them go. Go deep and find out some bad habits that you might be carrying onto your life or habits that you wish to get rid of. Ask yourself whether you want to let go of such habit or not.

2. Set a plan. Oftentimes it is difficult to get rid of bad habits without a plan. Be prepared for the worse and be prepared to try repeatedly until these bad habits are no more.

3. Make a list of all the reasons you want to quit your bad habits and make a list of all the things you will get out of it from quitting the bad habit.

Do your best in making such list a positive and truly impactful list and do your best in making the list very long. For example, if you want to stop binge eating, you will write a list of all the reasons why you want to quit and all the benefits you will gain from quitting the habit. Once you've established the list, you need to memorize it and absorb it into your mind. Visualize yourself where you have successfully quit the bad habit.

4. Take swift action to ending such bad habit. Now that you have identified the bad habits in your life start to take actions in stopping it. Whatever efforts you have taking place realize that none is wasted. Let's say that you have a bad habit of yelling at children, one way for you to act is to simply not talk and use written communication until you are calm down during such situations. Take as many actions you can into obliterating such habit.

5. Talk to somebody supportive about your determination to end such bad habit. Or ask advice from people who have experienced from such bad habit. If you have someone very supportive in your life, then you should consider expressing your need on getting rid of these habits. If you know someone who has previously suffered from certain habits and have conquered

it over, then, of course, you should ask for advice on how they have done it as well.

6. You will have ups and downs. Quitting a habit won't come right away, but you shouldn't give up on trying. When one person who tries to constantly end a bad habit fail repeatedly over time, it's common that they will start to give up and feel hopeless. Realize that you will have setbacks during your journey, but you should never give yourself up and keep going at it again and again until you succeed! If you really want to end such habit, you will continue in making efforts each time.

7. Reward yourself. Try to congratulate yourself or reward yourself with some prize in which you have successfully made some sort of attempt to end such habit. These prizes will only keep you more motivated and more captivated into the project. Start with small victories and go from there. Rewards can be as simple as favorite foods, favorite places, and even favorite activities.

By being aware of these steps, I am only sure that it will only help you move on away from these bad habits.

Chapter 7: Developing Uplifting Habits

It is always great to establish and develop only positive and productive habits that will only fuel us and make us more prone for future success. In many cases, clutter might have distracted you from thinking about and developing some positive habits that can make the difference between having a great day and having a bad day.

Some of these habits may seem so simple and obvious that we don't even think of implanting them regularly. Some of these habits may seem very weird and vulgar that you may not even try it without knowing it's benefits.

How Good Habits Can Change Your Life?

Good habits will help you on your way to success. But, there are many more benefits that will come which will completely change your life and you. Here are some of the few things that such positive and good habits can influence your life:

- Stress Avoidance

When healthy habits become part of your daily routine, then positive energy and positive acts will come naturally. You will find yourself with a reduce amount of stress levels. Having a good habit in planning your day in advance ensures that you are always in control of the situation. IT pays to always be on top of the situation, that way you control speed and direction of things. Habits are more like exercising in each day, starting your day off with a glass of lemon juice and taking time out to will keep your stress at bay.

- Confidence

These habits can give you that boost of confidence that you well needed. These habits will help you accept the person who you are and to accept the anxiety that you might be holding.

- Trust and Respect

With good and healthy habits, you make yourself a much more reliable person. And with reliability, it becomes a characteristic that is appreciated in all aspects of life. If you cultivate good habits, like the habit of always reaching on time, you are likely to be respected for it. When a client is faced with a multitude of options to employ from, the goodwill and reliability attached to your name will increase your chances of landing the job. Following a routine means that you are in control of your life, this leaves you with mind space to deal with other problems. When you enable yourself to inspect problems and provide solutions, you will find people wanting to work with you.

- Efficiency

Like I said earlier, practice makes perfect, routine is a daily practice. Good habits are pretty much daily practice in which it helps focusing you on regaining the chances at life. Get more done in less time. You can do that only if you master your primary skills and have a well-planned approach towards tackling your job. Don't put in unnecessary effort. They say that lazy people are the smartest because they always find a shortcut to finish their work. You don't need to be lazy; all you need to be is smart.

- Improvement in Health

Daily exercise obviously helps you improve your health. With good habits, replace the bad ones. Exercise on top of having cut down on smoking and drinking will see you becoming healthy as horse in no time. Waking up early every day is a habit that can improve your health. It will allow you to have meals earlier, prepare for your day much better, and give you more time to exercise.

TOP 5 BEST HABITS FOR A BETTER YOU

Smiling (Habit)

Smiling at yourself first thing in the morning and throughout your day to others is one of the most positive and most powerful habits that you can make. If only everybody in the world can understand what a simple smile can do.

As a matter of fact, when you look at yourself with a great big smile, you subconsciously and biochemically send out the message within yourself that you are confident and that you accept yourself for who you are.

Nothing great will ever happen if you consistently feel negative about yourself and never do anything about it. You must always keep a positive attitude and feel awesome all about life to live life to the fullest.

If you want to go, an extra step, just say, "I love you" to yourself, hug yourself if needed, give yourself a flying kiss and wish yourself good luck for the brand-new day that is ahead of you.

Journaling (Habit)

With this habit requires you to have a diary or digital device that is compatible for you to write down your feelings. It's more than simple; journaling can be fun and therapeutic.

So, here is how you start. You get a notebook, and you spend at least 5-minutes a day writing to yourself. Write completely whatever comes to your mind and now.

Taking the time to pause and figure out what to write about is distracting and will lead to procrastination.

Be open and be transparent. If you don't feel like writing anything, then write that If you don't have the time to do journaling then at least take a moment to mention that, just be honest with yourself. If after a few days the concept of journaling still seems difficult to tap into and completely outside of your comfort zone, just remember, this is a new habit, and it can be difficult to start out. But after a few attempt, it will come off natural.

Journaling can help you create a pathway from your inward self to your everyday life and help you realize your ultimate possibility. It can also help declutter your mind and clear up your mind.

Be Gracious (Habit)

Being grateful is one of the most generous actions anyone can make. As simple as it may sound, our minds may be so cluttered that we cannot take the moments to appreciate everything that we have. It may easy to list off as many things going wrong with our life, but how about listing everything good in life? There are millions of things that each one of us can feel grateful about. The life we live, your ability to read, the air we breathe, everything!

You can use your journal to help you. When you wake up write down three things that you are grateful for and continue to do so until it becomes part of your daily morning routine. I guarantee you that becoming gracious will change your life perspective on life. By doing this simple ritual even a person who has lived life with mediocrity will feel blessed and fortunate.

Nothing in life is to be taken for granted. Every little thing has infinite value, and we honor this value by becoming grateful for it. Simply having a life is worth being grateful for.

Be thankful for people and for your possessions.

The minute we become thankful and satisfied with what we have and with who we are, we can envision an even brighter future with even more opportunities to be thankful.

Using Your Envisioning Abilities (Habit)

Like I said in the beginning, your mind is your most powerful tool and you can use it entirely for you. But how? Well, that's with envisioning your future. Every one of us has a vision for ourselves. And every single day we must feel a step closer to our envisioned goals and dreams.

To become more productive, close your eyes and focus on the plans you have for your life. Do it every single morning and night. Sit down, and for 10 minutes, close your eyes and envision. Your thoughts are magnets, and it can attract whatever you focus your mind on.

All it takes is the solid belief that it will happen and that you are worth everything in the world. You can use this habit pretty much throughout your day, while you are driving before you sleep, when you are bored from work, or when you are spacing out watching television. Close your eyes and dream. Our dreams and future life are obviously more thrilling than the latest newsfeed or political news.

Try it right now, close your eyes and envision yourself. Who do you want to be? What does it look like? What kind of accomplishments did you settle? Envisioning helps bring hope, and hope is a way of manifesting faith. There's nothing to lose, nothing bad comes out of this. It will only make you happier and hopeful for what is to come.

Practice Compassion (Habit)

Most people have a huge ego rather than a bigger heart. Compassion is where the real joy of life is located. Our motives, opinion, and interests are often put in front of others because we struggle to be objective. Thinking about a situation objectively means to see both your sides and the other person's pointy of view.

Many people are focused on themselves because our main concern is always with loving ourselves first. There is certainly nothing wrong with loving yourself, which is what this book is all about. What we need to understand is that there is a fine line between loving yourself and respecting yourself. If you truly respect and love yourself, you understand the power that comes from being able to relinquish some of that egoism by turning it into compassion.

Build upon the love and respect that you feel for yourself and use it towards others as well. You will find that this compassion will only feed your soul and let you understand life in a broader sense.

Be prone in spreading only positive energy, not negative energy. Be compassionate to people, animals, and nature itself. Smile at people and let them know that you are there to help no matter who they are or what situation that they may be in. Help animals and be kind to them.

Learning the art of compassion and making it a habit of practice in daily life. You will change your overall perspective of life into a much more meaningful one.

There are many other worthwhile and productive things to do. Once you find your passion, you should pursue it and don't let anything get in your way. Only good and positive habits can replace the negative ones. Here is a short list of some other hobbies to keep in mind:

- Learn and play a musical instrument
- Master a new language
- Start a YouTube channel

- Learn how to paint and create art
- Learn and perform magic tricks
- Collect antiques or other cool stuff
- Play and engage in athletic activities
- Volunteer in helping charities
- Biking
- Hiking
- Surfing
- Swimming
- Reading every day
- Writing every day
- Watch and study movies and televisions
- Learn how to make a video game or an app
- Learn something new
- Write some music

Chapter 8: Procrastination

In this chapter, we will be talking about how you can completely end the destructive habit of procrastination to take charge of your life fully and to become more productive.

Letting Go of Procrastination and Fighting Against Distractions

Getting past procrastination is about being honest with yourself and being aware of procrastination. It is a confidence drainer. It is because you do not want to deal with or confront something that you fear

Procrastination is something that many of us struggle with every single day. We simply fail to find the motivation to undertake a task, project or activity because of the many executes, habits, thoughts and fears. Procrastination is very easy to overcome if we simply take the time to understand the dynamics this common past-time

Reasons for Procrastination

For every action, there is a cause – a trigger of sorts that instantly brings forth decisions and behaviors that lead to daily and lifelong consequences that any of us accept without questions.

For those of us who are not aware of these triggers, life can be very difficult to manage. On the other hand, those of us who are successfully able to identify these triggers as a cause of our procrastinating habits can indeed begin to take steps that will help us break free of these unproductive habitual cycles

Procrastination can also evolve through a set of interlinking childhood experiences that we naturally accepted into our psyche at an age and time when we knew no better. This very much involves unconscious experiences that we struggle with on a constant basis throughout our lives.

Getting past procrastination is about being honest with yourself, acknowledge where you have been procrastinating. Remember that this is not ok with you because it leaves you feeling disempowered and you want to build your self-confidence. Recognize that taking immediate action steps towards the things fear is one of the best ways to prevent and stop procrastination.

Pick one area where you have been procrastinating in your life and commit to taking three action steps over the next week. Tell at least one person in your life about the three action steps you committed to taking. Ask them to hold you accountable by following up with you and supporting you.

What Productive People Do

Productivity is all purposefully and consistently moving in the desired direction. Productivity is not doing lots of stuff fast. You can do plenty things and get nowhere closer to your ideal. Most people are living their lives this way. They are burning themselves out running in a million of different directions. Our society has become obsessed with constant doing. There's little time left for being and living.

Here is what it's like to become an insanely productive person.

1. **Productive people don't care what other people are doing.**

Most people spend most their time watching and observing other people. The goal is to emulate and copy or to compare and compete. This highlights an utter lack of achieved identity – an emotional and spiritual immaturity.

On the other hand, insanely productive people spend very little if any of their time worrying about what other people, "their competition" are doing. They see this as a distraction from their work. They put their heads down and execute

2. Productive people don't care what other people think

Many of the population lives in absolute fear about what other people think of them. They try to be perfect. They try to be liked. They are unwilling to be vulnerable. To be real and truthful

Insanely productive people put themselves completely out there. They are doing their work for themselves and for the people it was intended for. They are doing their work for themselves and for the people it was intended for. Anyone outside their target audience does not exist to them. Haters and critics are flowers, not darts.

3. Productive people care about who they serve

Though productive people don't' care about what other people think, they do care about the people they serve. They have a love for humanity that is nothing short of divine. Every person has infinite potential in his or her worldview. When they look at another person, they see a person – not an object. They feel.

Insanely productive people are incredibly empathetic. They relate to people on their level. They're relevant and connect. They influence with their love. Those they serve can feel it they're changed.

4. Productive people don't need permission.

Most people wait to launch their careers or to pursue their goal. They rather wait for that perfect opportunity. Most people believe that they can start after they have enough time, money, connections, and credentials. They wait until they feel "secure". Not insanely productive people.

Insanely productive people started last year. They started five years ago before they even knew what they were doing. They had started before they had any money. They had started before they had all the answers. They started when no one else believed in them. The only permission they needed was the voice inside them prompting them to move forward. And they moved.

5. Productive people learn through doing

Theory can only take a person so far in life. Putting yourself out there and falling flat on your face, over, and over, and over is how insanely productive people learn. Rather than having meeting and discussion, productive people will go out and practice.

While most people are reading, thinking, and dreaming, insanely productive people are out doing. The goal is to learn while creating output. Non-productive people, on the other hand, have a lopsided ratio of input and output – with very little of the latter.

Productive people enjoy where they presently are on the path.

Insanely productive people find joy in the journey. They aren't always waiting for that next chapter in life. They are happy with where they are. They are alive. Non-productive people wait for contentment until after they graduate from college, or get that promotion, or retire. All the while, their life passed them by and they never experienced the moment.

Productive people prune their lives

Insanely people continuously "clean and declutter their minds". They are minimalists! When life starts getting too busy, they step back and remove what is unneeded. Rather than adding more to their life, they say, "no" to almost everything. If they've made non-essential commitments in their future, they cancel those superfluous appointments. Their lives are simple and to the point.

Productivity is not what you do; it's who you are. It's less about life-hacks and more about lifestyle. You can learn all the tricks you want, but only the fundamentals performed consistently will quickly move your life to a much more impactful one.

METHODS TO STOP PROCRASTINATING

Procrastination is a deadly habit that may have its consequences over the long term. You must be careful and do not let this awful habit take valuable time of your life. Here are some steps that can help you overcome procrastination.

Break Your Tasks into Manageable Steps

You often procrastinate subconsciously because you find your work overwhelming for you. IT will be good to break your work into small parts and focus on one part of your job at a time. Try to make your tasks simple so that you can complete them quick, for instance, if you are writing a book, you can divide it into small manageable parts. Book writing is a full-scale project, and it can increase your procrastination. You can divide it into small phases, such as:

- Research work
- Selections of topics
- Create the structure/outline of eBook
- Draft the content
- Write chapter 1 to 12
- Revisions and proofreading, etc.

These steps can make your work manageable and increase your concentration. These small steps will help you to concentrate on each aspect of book writing.

Change your atmosphere

The atmosphere may have a greater impact on your productivity. Look at your room and work desk;

evaluate your feelings about your desk and room. Some environments make you feel sleepy and snuggle. Try to change your workspace and atmosphere to increase your motivation and inspiration for a long duration. Make sure to revamp your environment and remove all distractions around you.

Your work environment should motivate you to complete your job on time. IT may require some experimentation, and you can try to different places to select one production location. IF you want a place with fewer people around you, it will be good to work in your room. You can work in libraries as well to do work.

Employed people can't select perfect environment for working. In this case, you can modify your environment and remove all distractions around you. Carefully organize your work desk and decorate it with inspirational quotes and pictures. You can put one or two photo frames on your work desk. You can keep your favorite mug on your desk. Sometimes, you may not like the work assigned to you, but it doesn't mean to feel miserable. IF you can create home atmosphere, you will be able to inspire yourself to get all things done, even your hated tasks.

Detailed timeline with specific deadlines

Only one deadline for your project is a clear invitation to procrastination. Your mind will get the impression that you have time and push things again and again until it is too late. After breaking your project, you will know that you must complete every task by a particular date. Your time should be robust, such as if you are unable to finish all this by current day; it will jeopardize your other planning. You should strictly follow each deadline to avoid urgency acts. You must break down your task list and complete each task on a date to avoid the feelings of procrastination.

Eliminate Procrastination Pit-Stops

If you procrastinate too much, it can reduce your productivity. You must identify the bookmarks of your browser that may take lots of time. Try to shift them in the separate folder and disable automatic notifications of your email. IT is important to get rid of any distractions around you. Some people take drastic steps to deactivate or delete the Facebook accounts. This move is good to address extreme procrastination. You can do everything that reduces distractions around you, such as keep your mobile on silent, deactivate the e-email and Facebook notifications.

Hang out with people who can become your inspiration

If you spend only ten minutes with entrepreneurs, you will be made more inspired to do something big. Try to spend time with those people who are your inspiration. Try to identify your colleagues, friends, and individuals who can trigger you to hard work. Hang out with them, and soon you will be able to get rid of procrastination. These people increase your spirit and work drive. For instance, a career blogger can get good results by spending time with career development experts. You can communicate with them and share your problems.

A companion can make this whole procedure easy and funny for you. If your buddy can help you to set your goals, it will be a great thing for your success. Your friends should have his/her goals. You both can hold each other answerable for your plans and goals. It is not necessary to have the same goal, but you both can support each other to complete your work.

Set Your Priorities

You must set your priorities at the start of the day and follow an 80/20 rule. For instance, if you have ten items in a to-do-list, you should separate 2 or 3 most important things. Try to complete the most important task first and try to finish it first instead of focusing on others. If you have several smaller jobs to do, you should organize these jobs in a checklist and start with the most important projects.

It is called multi-task jobs, and one by one handling is called "single handling" it will help you to save your time and reduce the chances of conflicts. Planning will help you to increase 50 percent productivity.

Stay Away from Electronics

If you are completing important tasks in a limited period, you should keep yourself away from electronics, such as switch off the mobile phone, sign out of Twitter and Facebook. A phone call, email, message, and tweet will increase distractions, and you may not be able to focus on your work. Your focus should be on your job only and try to complete it professionally and without errors.

Set Your Goals

If you want to save time and increase your productivity, you should set your goals and focus on these aims. The goals will give you a pathway to work; therefore, you should think about your work and write down important things carefully. Your goals can be in the areas such as family, education, finances, health and other things. Your goal can be like "starting your own business" or opening a bookstore or getting an award.

At an initial level, your goal should be short-term to increase your motivations. It will be good to give a deadline to yourself and work hard to accomplish your goal within time limits. Start with baby steps because smaller steps will help you to move toward larger goals of life. For instance, if you wish to start a new business, you will start with the selection of a location and get a business license.

You may need to attend some classes to learn bookkeeping, recruiting process and other things. You should learn to manage your budget, for your business and create measurable goals and learn to remove difficulties in your way. Your goals should be realistic enough and keep track of your progress.

Manage Your Time

If you want to increase your productivity, it is important to manage our time and remove all distractions that can disturb your work. Make a list of tasks that are essential to accomplishing, and you should prioritize each task, such as:

- Task 01: due by 12 pm
- Task o2: due by 5 pm
- Task o3: due by tomorrow, 8pm
- So, on and so on

If you always have consistent tasks, select the most productive time of the day to do this task and try to complete your work at this stage. After completing each task, you should take a break to refresh yourself to increase focus. A break of 15 to 30 minutes is enough to stick to clear your mind and look forward to another task. It will increase your productivity and speed.

Keep track of your regular progress and mark all complete tasks. It will increase a sense of accomplishment and increase your motivation. You should regulate your works and rewrite your list of priorities on a regular basis. You should have some time for fun because it can refresh your mind. You may sleep for 7 to 8 hours because it is necessary on a regular basis to keep you energetic and alert.

Procrastination means postponing or delaying your tasks. It is a tendency to increase fear, heightened anxiety, and self-consciousness. If you want to increase your productivity and to declutter your mind fully, you must get rid of distractions and procrastinating habits. It is an easy way for any of us to get stuck and end up having an emotional breakdown over unfinished duties.

The worst part is that sometimes, we don't even realize we are procrastinating since it often comes in the form of "taking a break" or "getting inspiration" or thinking that I can do it later, etc. You can get rid of procrastination or make it productive with proper planning.

Chapter 9: Willpower

In this chapter, we will learn how we can use willpower to get anything that we want in life. Sounds quite impossible, isn't it? There is a saying about the main quality of inventors and innovators that underlines that, when all others know that something is impossible or cannot be achieved, the inventors simply don't know that. Hence, they have the mind uncluttered and so they can invent. The problem with many people is that they are often feeling unmotivated and do not want to spark a change in life. We all have had our moments when we only dreamt about lying in bed for the rest of our lives. When people feel like, it is obvious that they won't be able to get what they want or need, like most motivated and determined people do. The worse thing is, those who feel unmotivated continue to tell themselves that life is not fair and blame the others for their lack of energy and eagerness. That way of thinking is not going to get them nowhere, obviously!

When you look at it from a larger perspective, willpower is not only an instrument that helps us when in need to achieve something but a habit of our decluttered mind that knows how to manage resources in order to get gratification.

To better understand this concept, we could look at small kids. Even though they lack experience and skills, their willpower is unbreakable. They are so honest in what they want, and they have such litter clutter affecting their mind (close to clutter, we could say) that sometimes their willpower is stronger than that of the parents together. It is well established that there are many lessons we could learn directly by observing little children. The way they go for what they feel is good for them, the way they treat obstacles with such determination and bravery, their lack of worrying about eventual outcomes, it is a thing of beauty that makes us, the adults, have hope.

To conclude the parallel with a kid's approach to life, in terms of will power, we must say that being motivated and resilient is not just for some of us. While it's true that some standout and excel at this – for example, those who perform in sport – motivation acts as a switch. If we set our mind to it, it comes by effortlessly. If we doubt it, we never find it.

As the famous writer Mark Twain use to say, "All you need in this life is ignorance and confidence, and then success is sure". Exactly what a child has naturally, isn't it? He ignores failure, he has no clue about what could go wrong, hence being full of confidence.

Successful people are only successful because they were willing to work for it. If you are going to work for it, you need to know how to do that and still have time for your passions and interests. Only the lucky ones get to engage in what they love and achieve success. For the vast majority, success is a result of some combined skills and a healthy mindset, lots of self-discipline and hard work. A decluttered mind will find it easy and enjoyable to engage in hard activities and nail them, for it will strive to achieve the higher gratification possible. We all know that the higher we climb, the better the view.

On a more pragmatic note, there are some similarities we could easily observe when analyzing successful people and their way of doing things.

- They take on the hardest challenges.
- They have little to no fear of failure, on the contrary, they embrace failure and learn from it.
- They have strong work ethics.
- They mix between self-sacrifice and comfort, without choosing one or the other drastically.
- They know and accept openly what they don't know or can't do. This way they can easily improve.
- They never lie about themselves nor the others.
- They usually help others for they know that at some point they will be in need of help too.
- They value discipline, even though they don't obsess over it. As it's the case with many of these

characteristics, if exaggerated they could easily become detrimental rather than helpful.
- They have solid criteria for judging their progress.
- They stay as objective as possible and rely on non-subjective opinion regarding themselves or their activity.
- They value friendship and humanity.
- They do not want success at all costs, and they won't sacrifice their souls for achieving it.

It is merely impossible for a cluttered mind to be able to develop in such a way that it achieves some of these characteristics listed above. This we can be sure of. Therefore, in order to switch on your willpower, you should be positive about what your resources are, be honest and frank about your skills and capabilities and plus, be sure your mind is at peace with itself.

Building up on a solid foundation is a key point to achieving a resistant and gratifying result in the end. There's this saying I heard years ago about the act of trying, that I usually tell people when they ask how to start, how to get yourself motivated enough to begin. It goes something like this: Try and fail but don't fail to try.

Chapter 10: Investing in Yourself

You'll hear it said that the best investment you can make isn't in stocks or bonds. Instead, it's in yourself. But have you thought about what it really means to invest in yourself? I'll give you a hint: It's not about the money. In fact, money should be the least of your worries at this point.

Most people think that "invest in yourself" is just another way of saying "go back to school and get a degree" or "spend money on a conference". And while you could do those things to some degree of success, investing in yourself is not about spending money or taking classes per se. It is, actually, much more than that.

Investing in yourself is about looking at your life to see what areas you could be doing better in and what areas you'd just plain old like to explore, and then taking the time to do so. And that's not limited to formal education, by any means.

As a matter of fact, nowadays formal traditional education tends to show its limits all around the globe. Not only it isn't enough to build up a meaningful life and achieve happiness, but it also contributes to ones lack of orientation and ability to invest in those areas that would require a special attention. Even more so, even though it takes care of the most basic skills, it rarely boosts one's true potential. How so?

Since we were little kids, we were taught to derive our sense of self from some form of authority – teachers, tutors –; at the same time, we got used always to compare ourselves with others to understand our own value. When we prepared hard for an exam, we expected to get a high mark. For most, this was the end of learning. Once we achieved the appreciation of the teacher, we considered our learning process has stopped.

Many of today's studies regarding education from early ages reveal that this approach does more harm than good. Self-developing, constant learning new things, keeping curiosity at high levels, and much more, are related not to rewards, but to the realization that one's possibilities are infinite and absolutely everyone is capable of taping in their potential. Regardless of the ability to follow the rules or adapt to objective criteria, each individual contains the ever-old urge to improve, find out more about the world around, educate and prosper.

This is what investing in one self actually means. Resources like time, mind focus, intellectual effort or physical activities are the most important asset you use when investing. The return of investment is way more than anyone can predict when starting the process.

Even though it seems it's not rocket science, when faced with our options, it becomes a difficult task actually to do it. The most popular excuses we are all familiar with are lack of time, other obligations, lack of energy and others. Sound familiar, isn't it?

The mind cluttering is, as you've seen many times before throughout the reading of this book, one of the biggest enemies when faced with the possibility of investing in oneself and improving.

You have to know from the beginning that our minds don't do well with new and unpredictable, and fear the unknown. Therefore, the main impulse we usually feel is to keep it safe, to rest within our boundaries, never to leave our comfort zone. When the cluttering phenomena happens, the mind not only tries to maintain comfort, but it also finds excuses and actually demotivates us. Some of those excuses are referred to in detail throughout this book.

Some famous brand of sports clothing had one of the most successful advertising slogans, and I'm positive we are all familiar with. It was simple, efficient, motivational and... true. The insight was suitable for everybody, not only for people who engage in physical activities. We want to borrow this piece of genius and use it against whatever obstacles may occur when you are close to investing in yourself: "Just do it!"

What Does It Mean to Invest in Yourself?

What comes to mind when you hear the word investing? Does it mean, putting your money in insurance, mutual funds, the stock market or even high-yield investments? Other people might only think about investing when they are about to die, and they haven't left anything for their offspring.

Be yourself, and do what you can to make yourself the best you can be. Everyone's life is about the book they are reading at the moment. That's what happens because of the next occasion for doubt, or anger, or jealousy, or fear, or brain dumps, are just around the corner. Then life returns to the before temp-buzz paths.

Many people even invest heavily in health supplements, personal trainers and beauticians to make themselves live longer, healthier or even look younger! Imagine the advertising budget for beauty companies nowadays.

The most important and No.1 rule is to "Invest in Yourself. If you don't, who else will?

Your parents will only invest in your education only until you leave college. But that is just the basic necessities provided and does not teach you important lessons about financial education.

Would you depend on colleges or universities to teach you how to make money? Most colleges only teach you skills so you can earn money working for other people. How about business school? Honestly, if business lecturers are such experts at business, why are they still lecturing there instead of making a fortune in business ventures?

Would your boss teach you how to succeed in business so that one day, you will be in his position?

You and only you have to be proactive enough to take that responsibility.

You see, when you invest in yourself, it means taking on the importance of educating yourself. Education not in the academic or technical sense, though they are necessary skills to be developed in life. Our education does not and should not stop at college.

For most working adults, their education enters retardation stage after they leave college. They stop learning, and therefore they stop growing. They only grow sideways from eating too many pizzas or take-out during their busy lunch breaks.

We know that IQ is important right? But why aren't the most intelligent people in the world the richest people in the world? There are many accountants and financial planners rushing to their cars every evening trying to beat the after work traffic congestions! They are not rich!

So how is investing in yourself done?

Daydream a little.

Start by daydreaming a little. What have you always wanted to try? Now's the time to schedule exactly that — whatever it is. Skydive, get up a half hour early every day to write that Great American Novel, visit a local attraction that you've always been curious about but never stopped in at — whatever.

Taking the time to do something that you've always wanted to do is a way of showing yourself that YOU are important. You'll feel more energetic and just better in general. Like that old commercial says, "you're worth it!".

Learn a new skill.

Yes, this could involve taking a class. (Why did I wait decades to start learning oil painting finally?) But it could also mean reading up on a subject using books from the library, or downloading a French podcast and practicing every day. Or it could mean joining a knitting club for beginners and learning together in a group. Heck, it could even mean actively trying to improve your score in the latest smart phone game craze.

The point is to do something new that takes practice and effort. Exercising your brain helps keep it sharp, and makes life a whole lot more interesting.

Get over an old stumbling block.

We all have things that are holding us back, keeping us from being the people we really could be if we worked through an issue. Maybe you worry all the time or are incredibly shy but long to have friends. Or maybe your checking account is constantly overdrawn and you and your spouse are always fighting about money.

It's time for a change. Get counseling, get therapy, get whatever it takes to get over that old stumbling block and move past it. It's one investment that will be WELL worth it.

Make healthy habits.

Eat well, get enough sleep (no burning the candle at both ends!), and exercise daily (for example, by taking a daily walk.) Healthy habits give you the energy to DO the things you want to do, rather than being run down and sick. There's nothing like literally taking care of yourself to improve the quality of your life.

Give yourself a break.

Finally, one of the most overlooked ways to invest in yourself is to just plain old give yourself a break. If you're so over-scheduled that you're constantly stressed out from rushing here and there, cancel something. You (and your family members) do NOT need to do everything. No one will be scarred for life if they aren't busy every single moment. We all need breaks, and you are no exception. Massages and stuff are great, but simply doing nothing is an awesome break too. When was the last time you scheduled a do-nothing day?

The last thing remaining after you get into the habit of reading, listening and associating is to implement everything you have learned. Don't let these tasks intimidate you and start applying one step at a time. Just like Rome wasn't built in a day, it will take the time to accumulate knowledge and act upon it. But it is a critical step because no knowledge will ever bring any result unless it is acted upon. To know and not to do is not to know!

So, start now to invest in yourself, develop the essential skills for success and earn the greatest return you ever will. Here's to your success!

How to Achieve What You Want in Life

If you have a dream, a big and audacious goal that you want to achieve, you will need a set of appropriate skills. You can find thousands of tips on this subject, for example, 25 most important skills or 100 best ways to achieve anything and so on, but nowhere else will you find a simple list of 2-3 most important skills which when prioritized, will guarantee your desired result. Why is that? Because very few know about it and those that do – well they want to keep it a secret or share it with few.

I have been compiling this knowledge bit by bit throughout my entire life, always applying these simple yet tremendously effective principles and I would like to leave this experience for posterity and all those who will listen. It is the most gratifying and special feeling one can achieve, to be able to participate in the well-being of his fellows. I have nothing to hide because only a few of you will be able to listen and apply these principles, unfortunately. Only those who can truly hear and understand! On the other hand, the fact that you make an effort to acquire knowledge puts you in a very good place. As hard as it is to believe, there are not so many like you.

The independent thinker

FIRST, the most important skill is the skill of self-education and the ability to think independently. It is required to be able to understand how everything works. By everything I mean first and foremost – the life itself. What is life and what is the purpose of creation? What are the fundamental laws of the Universe? What is the purpose of your life? How do people behave and how can you interact with them effectively? What is love? What is money and how does it work? What are the basic laws of life, human relationships, money, success, and happiness?

To learn these things and know how to apply them in life, one is required to use the principles of self-directed education. No formal education will help here. In reality, that's not even its goal. No one will give you such knowledge and skills unless you have the desire to acquire them for yourself. On the contrary, people will always try to lower you to their level. And practically no one knows what life is and how to control it effectively.

To know how to think independently means to know how to fill your mind with light, positive thoughts, useful ideas, to have a "builder" mindset despite the tendency of a small but very aggressive number of people towards negativism, "wrecker" mentality, condemnation and argument. By thinking independently and consistently educating yourself, you will inevitably find understanding of the creation, the Creator, the purpose of establishment and your role in creating your reality. It will make you healthy and will teach you to actually love others which in itself could be enough for a successful and a happy life.

The skill for self-education and the ability to think independently are two separate skills. I have combined them only because they cannot be developed separately from one another. They are connected by an absolute belief that only a few know the truth and that almost everything in our world had been made up. Formed by those who reap the most benefit from it. Perhaps, your benefit is in something else. Look for the truth yourself; find it in the most unexpected places. Create or find such a system of beliefs that reflects the reality to the limit. For that is essential!

Remember that your system of beliefs or what you believe in is your greatest guide in life. Everything you believe in becomes your reality, so it is vital to believe in correct principles, in something that is indeed true. Majority of people today believe in made up things without even realizing it. They fight demons and phantoms. Therefore, they can never control their lives. Look for the truth, and you will find it! Do not allow anyone brainwash you, and by someone, I mean traders, politicians, religious fanatics and so-called "scientists." Today it has become so familiar to trust science, refer to scientific research although modern scientists have created more "demons" than any sorcerers or voodoo men. Get your personal testimony of everything that you're learning and build your system of beliefs based on such foundation.

Be true to your desires

SECOND, no less important skill is to know exactly what you want out of life. Determine what you want first, second, and so on and so forth? What price are you willing to pay? You either pay up front, for example by stepping out of your comfort zone, with your time and hard work, or you pay later, for instance by losing your freedom, friends, family, health or with total disappointment in life. Always think of the consequences! If you don't know what you want out of life, it will be filled with incidents, and not very pleasant ones at that. Therefore, plan your life or else someone will plan it for you! The best method of planning is to design on paper (in writing). Dreams, pondering, prayers, meditations, visualizations – THESE are important. However, anything not written down remains unrealized or will be realized not enough as desired.

The feedback policy – think & act

THIRD, a very significant skill to achieve practically any goal is to apply the cycle of achievement which includes the ability to think and the ability to act. Usually, people either have the capacity to work (the vast majority of them), or they have the potential to think (a small minority of them) and even fewer possess both abilities. This is a very simple principle that is always successfully when used by intelligent automated machines, sometimes insects, and also some animals. It is called feedback policy. Results always speak for themselves. The following is a simple cycle of achieving the desired result: goal – action – result – analysis of the effect – work. Keep going until you get the result that you want. Usually, people can't do this. They get caught up with "demons" and phantoms that had been made up by someone else or stumble because of an already cluttered mind. Those that can – achieve tremendous results in their life.

The ability to think big, creatively and at the same time to be able to focus on a goal is not an easy task. Therefore, learning is required. For starters, you would need to master certain thinking tools – concentration, visualization and mind-mapping is the necessary minimum. Planning on paper and not just in your head using a mind map allows you to learn to think efficiently, intelligently and so fast that no other genius of the past can ever compare.

Never stop. Affirm and visualize.

FOURTH, an essential skill for achieving goals is to learn to find strenght in yourself and discard any and all excuses and persevere to the end! By using the third power described above (the cycle of achievement) and observing how one comes up with all kinds of excuses not to do anything, learn to discard such excuses and persevere to the end. Affirmations and visualizations can help here.

Of course, this isn't a complete list of skills but is sufficient to achieve practically any realistic goal. The ability to communicate effectively can also be added to this list although for some it is one of the innate qualities or is developed within the family. If you were not gifted in this area, self-education and knowledge of the important laws of communication could help you.

The Golden Rule

One of those laws is so called the Golden Rule: "Do unto others as you would have them do unto you." You just need to remember that it is not just a mere wish or a good rule of behavior in society, but it is one of the most relentless laws of the universe. Because people will always treat you the way, you treat them. Lying, deceit, hypocrisy, violence, stealing, poverty and sickness in your life are the result of your dishonesty, disrespect, deceit, greed and hatred for others. In the same respect, joy, health, abundance, success and happiness is the result of your love and selfless service to others. This type of service is the key to prosperity, personal growth, and happiness. Make it your habit. Serve everyone you meet – at home, at work, at play.

Service, however, doesn't mean doing their job instead of them. Make service part of your mental attitude. Whatever you do, don't do it because you must, not out of obligation, not for money or any future benefit. Do it because of the joyful desire to serve those you love, which means virtually everyone you meet. Such mental attitude on its own can fill your life with prosperity and love. Just remember that the greatest source of love is YOU!

Minimalist Living

In this section, we will go over why you might really want to consider becoming a minimalist and the many benefits that derive from it. Of course, this entire book is about living the minimalist lifestyle and to therefore be able to declutter your mind for the best. So, let's get into it.

Minimalism can be simply defined as a way to put a stop to the gluttony of the world around us. It's the opposite of every advertisement we see plastered on the radio, TV or on the web. We live in a society that prides itself on the accumulation of stuff; we are fed up with consumerism, obsess about material possessions, accumulating debt, dwelling in distractions and never-ending noise. What we don't seem to have is any meaning left in our world as we know it.

By adopting a minimalist lifestyle, you can start by throwing out what you don't need in order to focus on what you do actually need. I know firsthand how little we actually need to survive. I was fortunate enough to live in a van for four months while traveling throughout Australia. This experience taught me many valuable lessons about what really matters and how little we really need from all this stuff we surround ourselves with.

Less is more

Living a minimalist lifestyle is all about reducing what can be reduced. There are a few obvious benefits such as less cleaning and stress, a more organized household and more money to be found, but there are also a few deep, life-changing benefits. What we don't usually realize is that when we reduce, is that we actually reduce a lot more than just stuff. If anything, the constant struggle of accumulating more and more things is a certain path to mind cluttering. Studies have shown that after a certain level of satisfaction is achieved when buying something, there is a certain decrease in satisfaction that eventually tends to get to zero. The economists call it marginal satisfaction. The most common example they use to explain this concept is pretty easy to grasp: think about the most amazing cake you can possibly imagine. Before you have it, you are susceptible to manifest a strong desire to eat that cake. After the first bite, you feel a great deal of satisfaction. The second bite can keep a high level of satisfaction but at some point the pleasure you feel from eating the cake slowly decreases. When you buy the same cake for the second time, a much lower degree of satisfaction is to be expected. The same happens with all possessions, no matter the origin.

The power of advertising makes it, so it is almost impossible for an individual to resist the urge of buying more and more things. They sell the projected satisfaction you will feel, but they never follow-up, after you actually buy the product.

Create room for what's important

When we purge our junk drawers and closets, we create space, and we also connect to a certain peace. If I would pick a comparison, the one that comes at hand, and that I also referred to in the introductory chapter of this book is the mouse-wheel or the marry-go-round. The cluttering phenomena occurs when we fail to resist the powerful stream of our society, and we engage in this intense and depleting rhythm of constant buying with less and less satisfaction and perspective. If we make room for what is really important, assuming we realized what that is, we lose that claustrophobic feeling, and we can actually breathe again. Create the room to fill up our lives with meaning instead of stuff is one of the most efficient ways to declutter and put an end to self-exhaustion.

More freedom

The constant and continuous accumulation of stuff is like an anchor; it ties us down and adds up to the pressure we feel on a daily basis. Imagine you work for three months and save money to buy an expensive gadget. After enjoying it for some time, not only the satisfaction you get from it decreases, but there's a new development that arises – we get attached to that object and we slowly but surely develop the fear of losing it. If we are honest, we realize that, in different degrees, we are always terrified of losing our 'stuff'. Manage to let it go, and you will experience freedom like never before: freedom from greed, debt, obsession and overworking. Even more so, chances are the cluttering cannot creep in that easily.

Focus on health and hobbies

When you spend less time at Home Depot trying unsuccessfully to keep up with the Joneses, you create an opening to do the things you love, things that you never seem to have time for. And the examples are so many we could write an entire new book only by compiling examples of wasted time doing incredibly unimportant things. We all have been there, secretly wishing the 24 hours' day would transform into 48 hours one, just for us, without anyone else to know. But then, if that would become true, who could guarantee that we wouldn't still spend all the time we have doing all sorts of insignificant things that, at most, give us the illusion that we feel good.

Everyone is always saying they don't have enough time, but how many people really stop and look at what they are spending their time doing? It's somewhat funny, but it seems that there is no time to just stop. You could be enjoying a day with your kids, hitting up the gym, practicing yoga, reading a good book or traveling. Whatever it is that you love you could be doing, but instead you are stuck at Sears shopping for more stuff. Frustrating, isn't it?

Less focus on material possessions

All the stuff we surround ourselves with is merely a distraction, we are filling a void. Money can't buy happiness; we all know the saying. But it can buy comfort. After the initial comfort is satisfied, that's where our obsession with money should end. Unfortunately, that is exactly where it all begins, for it is mainly a classic case of buying into an illusory comfort. Let's see this from a different perspective. Imagine you are hungry. Then, imagine your brain thinks that you eat, but your body doesn't get the nutritional substances it needs. For some time, because of the illusion that takes place inside your mind, you don't feel hungry anymore. After that illusion brakes, and they all do eventually, not only that you feel hungrier than before, but chances are you now feel sick also, exhausted, depleted. The same happens with the illusory filling of the void many of us feel.

It's hard not to get roped into the consumerism trap. I also need constant reminders that it's all a false sense of happiness. I have moments when I enjoy stuff, but I also recognize that I don't need it, sometimes at the same time I'm enjoying them.

We are bombarded by the media presenting promises of happiness through materialistic measures. Their instruments and capabilities are far more advanced than we think they are. Plus, it is a known fact that ethics is not the strong point of this domain. Therefore, it's no wonder we struggle every day. The best advice is to resist those urges, even though it seems hard. If we all realize that this is an empty path, that won't make us happy, we have a good starting point.

More peace of mind

When we cling onto material possessions, we create stress because we are always afraid of losing these things. By simplifying your life, you can lose your attachment to these things and ultimately create a calm, peaceful mind.

The less things you have to worry about, the more peace you have, and it's as simple as that.

More happiness

When de-cluttering your mind and, by extension, your entire life, happiness naturally comes because you gravitate towards the things that matter most. From being this final seemingly unreachable goal, happiness transforms into an obvious conclusion. You see clearly the false promises that resides in all the clutter, and you feel like you have finally broken the shield against life's true essence.

You will also find happiness in being more efficient, you will find concentration by having refocused your priorities, you will find joy by enjoying slowing down your pace and rhythm.

Less fear of failure

When you look at Buddhist monks, they have no fear, and they have no fear because they don't have anything to lose, nor to gain, for that matter

In whatever you wish to pursue doing you can excel, if you aren't plagued with the fear of losing all your worldly possessions. Obviously, you need to take the appropriate steps to put a roof over your head, but also know that you have little to fear except fear itself. The cluttering, as we settled already, feed itself on our fear, and there are little to no mental mechanisms that could help us in this regard. What does help, as we keep stating throughout the book, is knowledge, awareness and perspective. If anything, courage is built up by accessing this particular know-how and never let it go.

More confidence

The entire minimalist lifestyle promotes individuality and self-reliance. Nevertheless, it doesn't promote individualism, selfishness, the inflation of one's ego. Nowadays, more and more fellows get caught in this pattern, that develops the ego and underestimates the others. True confidence in your self has nothing to do with diminishing others. On the contrary. As stated clearly in a previous chapter of this book, helping others and trying your best to service them to the best of your abilities is the path to self-confidence. This assumed effort of positioning towards the others will make you more confident in your pursuit of happiness.

How to Become a Minimalist?

I wish I could tell you that all you have to do is throw the things you don't need or use, but things are a lot complicated than that – on the other hand, it's not like you see people living on a few things everywhere you look.

At the same time, there is hardly any method that could apply to each and every one. We are different, and these differences show up even more so when we look at how we deal with the excess of things surrounding us.

One of the most counterintuitive and solid pieces of advice I have for you is this: make friends with your hoarding habits.

As our perspective goes throughout the entire book, we emphasize that in order to get over something, you must first know what you are dealing with.

Keep, throw, sell, donate.

Go through your wardrobe, your books, even your memories and all the other stuff and build up piles, categories: what you're keeping, what you're throwing, what you're selling and what you're donating.

Clothes, for example any item that hasn't been worn for two years, should go into one of the above-mentioned categories. The chances of you wearing it again are a lot lower than are those of you being eaten by moths.

Try to find a higher purpose for this action, something that will further motivate you. If you ask me, the act of giving to the ones that are not as fortunate, in the form of a donation to charity is the best option out there.

Enter second hand groups on the internet, maybe organize a garage sale for all your friends. If the item is too out fashioned, make a good deed and donate it to someone who specializes in creating new, functional clothes for those in need from the material of old clothes.

After you got rid of the clothes you didn't wear, organize your wardrobe and make your aesthetic sense happy by admiring the result – it is finally the end of the never-ending chaos in your closet.

You never thought it was possible, did you?

As the case presents itself, one of the symptoms of mind cluttering that I discover more often than I would like to admit, is this: people get emotionally attached to items, objects, all sort of stuff. The concept of emotional value is circling around the way we associate some objects with what they resemble, or with what kind of memory it makes us recall.

One of the most intriguing yet effective solution for this problem presented itself to me when having a conversation about this topic with an old man I met at an art exhibition, many years ago. He was writing down words similar to what tags or keywords are, nowadays, on the internet, in his own notebook.

When, after a while, I enquired him about his practice, he told me that he creates memories by association. One or two words for every painting he liked, one or two words for every art object he loved. He said this is his unique way of following his passion of collecting amazing pieces of art.

I was stunned by his vision, and I could never forget his notebook, that had many words scribbled on it, and yet seemed incredibly valuable.

Find your own way

There are many ways in which you could, eventually, start walking the path to minimalist living style. One thing is certain, though: as you do it, the positive effect it has on your mind increases exponentially. A little space at the beginning is slowly but surely about to become a huge deal of freedom in the end.

Being free from the tyranny of possessions is a certain path to your mind's decluttering process, and thus I urge everyone to at least try this endeavor to see what it brings.

How to Feel Empowered In your Life

We covered almost everything that is required to declutter your mind and to take control in your life. Now here are some simple steps you can take to regain that glow of excitement onto your life. You can start with one, and slowly move on to the next.

1. You must be passionate about the things you do.

Being passionate is the most natural way for creating enthusiasm. Doing the great things that you are passionate about always provide yourself with motivation. You may be asking yourself an inquiry like, how can I become excited about something I am not passionate about? Well, you cannot force passion. Passion is something that you deliberately choose and develop over the long term; it's something that is given to you at birth.

2. You must show that you are visibly enthusiastic.

Knowing that one person is enthusiastic just by their body language is a clear shot to enthusiasm. This step requires you to work on your physical appearance and using positive gestures to suggest to the world that you are excited about what you do in life. People look at you and study your posture and body language and how you say things. You must be aware of your outward appearance to communicate those of enthusiasm.

To show that you are enthusiastic you should hold in natural energy. Don't act like you've drunk a gallon of coffee, just be at your best all the time. Get plenty of shut-eye and focus on the things that matter. Establish yourself a morning ritual that destines yourself to a fantastic life. Keep up on your hygiene and always smile as this conveys a positive message to all.

3. You must know your strengths and weaknesses.

Become aware of all your strengths and all your weaknesses. Now weaknesses are nothing to be ashamed of. Every one of us has unique strengths and weaknesses that create the person we are today. Acknowledge your weaknesses, and build upon your strengths. The things that you are good at will harness enthusiasm. This is the part where you continue to grow and learn from your mistakes. And as well for growth to occur, keep on working and reading about your problematic areas in your life and turn your weaknesses into strengths.

4. You must be yourself.

People are most enthusiastic when they are themselves. For you to become excited, you must set yourself free, be at peace with yourself and stop attending to everyone's need. At work, you must do your duties with happiness, speak your mind, share your views, and open your heart without the fear of being laid off or being judged.

People will have a perspective either way. Stop letting other people's limitations affecting you, rise above the bashing and the compliments to understand who you are. People always have this fear of being themselves at worst, but you need to apply some logic to that thinking. What is the most unfortunate thing that can happen for being you at work? Will they fire you because you love singing to the top of your lungs on the way to work?

5. You must be creative.

Creativity will put together your enthusiasm and produce an even greater amount of success. It is also the fastest way you can become enthusiastic. You can accomplish anything you want if you think outside of the box and execute it with enthusiasm. When you nurture your creativity, it helps along your passions and gives you a good layout for your future.

To be creative, you must encircle yourself with the loads' amount of inspiration. Inspiration leads to discovery and discovery leads to new things and experiences. Stop talking about all the creative ideas you have embodied in your mind and start developing it! Put your thoughts into words, then put your words into visuals. When people see your vision, they will take you seriously and will want to participate amongst this development.

6. You must have a positive mindset.

It is easy to be consumed by the negative emotions and chaotic things that come with life. By having a positive mindset at work, you are choosing to remain faithful and optimistic about the things that happen.

Ongoing resentment is only depriving us of the attitude and spirit that tells you that there is no future for you. You have a choice of whether you want to blame your circumstances on other people or accept the responsibility. It all starts with you. Are you in conversations of gossip or are you in discussions that focus on growth? What you surround yourself, you become. To become enthusiastic, you should keep a positive attitude, embrace the good things out of life.

7. You must be energetic.

Enthusiasm is linked to our energy levels. Therefore, it is relevant to take charge of ourselves and provide our bodies and brain with plenty of power. You cannot be excited if you are always feeling deprived and exhausted. Do your best to remain healthy as the best you can and adapt to a healthier lifestyle, choose the right foods, drink plenty of water, and exercise on a regular basis and you will improve productivity and your chances of bringing greats amount of energy and enthusiasm into your life very soon.

Some people have this myth that enthusiastic people are born that way. In some cases, yes. But the clear majority of passionate people are individuals who thrive to become excited. Many people had taken the incentive to walk on the path to enthusiasm. It is a deliberate choice and must not be taken lightly. It is entirely possible for you to achieve a much more exciting life, it all begins with you harnessing your attitude.

Changing Your Mentality

How frequently do you get unhappy or do you feel unenthusiastic about life? What is your meaning of happiness? Take this moment to answer that question.

Now life is all filled with many wonders and issues. But the actual purpose of life is to be happy and enthusiastic about life and everything that it must offer. Remember when you were a kid and all the things in life that made you happy, when you got a little bit older you most likely forgot the little things in life. Life was probably an adventure to you when you were a child, but why isn't it for you right now? Get into this concept that you are already happy, you just aren't acutely aware of it.

We must get back to our default state of happiness and be open to the things and offerings that life must offer to have an outlook of enthusiasm. Happiness can be something that some gain instantly, but it is something that some people must achieve and discover for themselves over the long -term.

Enthusiasm is necessary if you ever want to accomplish anything of value. You can have a loads amount of excitement within your life. This is the enthusiasm mentality; this is what it means to become a very enthusiastic person in life, at work, and in spirit. Let's go in.

How to Find Your Passion?

You will frequently hear me talking about passion throughout the course of this book, but for you to have any level of enthusiasm, you must have a passion for what you may be doing if you are looking for excitement in your life. You need to be thoroughly interested in work. Passion is your answer to great amounts of enthusiasm, it's what feeds your enthusiasm and makes it hungry for more, even during the hard times we all go through, it will help you face it with bold strength. To summarize, if you love what you do, excitement will come your way. For some, it's very hard for them to discover their passion so I wish to give you some advice on how you can find your real love of life.

Ask yourself: what puts a smile on my face?

Is there anything that makes you smile? Anything hint of a smile at either a job or at a hobby can indicate that you may be passionate about it. Following what makes you happy is a wonderful way to figuring out your life's purpose. Think about something that you do or brings you total peace when you do it. Peace accumulates happiness, and happiness brings about your passion.

Ask yourself: what seems natural to you?

In many cases, the things that come to us the easiest are things we are passionate about. It's very hard to dislike a job or a hobby that is very easy for you! For example, let's say you are naturally gifted at playing football, you find the activity easy, and this is fun for you. This leads to your passion. So, think back on everything that you do, whatever it is that comes off to you easy and fun, and this may very well be your passion. Remember, anything can be your passion. You can make a fantastic career out of anything you are passionate about.

Ask yourself: what makes you creative?

Think about something in your life where it expands your mind and something where you are always conjuring with unique, entertaining and interesting ideas relating to that subject. Whatever makes you creative is most likely something that you are very passionate about. For instance, if you are enthusiastic about art you can up with different paintings and different methods on how to practice art. If you are excited about music, you can up with different songs and develop your musical talents from there. Your passion is closely related to your creativity.

Ask yourself: what will you do for free?

Today, we often perceive that our passion relies on wealth. That if you want to be enthusiastic about something, you must make sure you can make money from it. No, that's not the way your world should lead. The problem with many people today is that they will rather head towards money than to work on themselves and do the things they've truly love. There are many examples of extremely successful people leaving their high-paying occupations to follow what they love. Why? Because if you truly follow what you genuinely love, it makes you rich from within. To firstly become wealthy on the outside, you must become rich from the inside. Doing what you have a passion for can lead to greatness and success. Many of the most successful people in the world got to where they are because they love what they do. So, think about something that you will do for only a penny and think about something you can do for the rest of your life.

Ask yourself: what do I enjoy talking about?

You will rather be more engaged in conversations where you are entirely interested in, and with this, you can find what you enjoy and what you are passionate about in life? For example, whenever you talk to some of your friends, and you see them rambling on and on about the same subject, then you can infer that they are passionate about that subject. If you can recall about the things you talk about, then approach your supportive friends, coworkers, and family and ask them what do you talk about the most. The response you'll get will surprise you and brighten your eyes. Try it out, it's a very insightful exercise and one that directs you closer to figuring out your passion.

Ask yourself: what makes me fearful of failure?

We often avoid pursuing our dream life because of the fear of failure; we often believe that there is no purpose pursuing the life we want to live because we will fail anyways. However, that's not the mentality of an enthusiastic person? An enthusiastic person is already lucky, as mention the janitor example in the first chapter. If you want to discover out where your true passions rely in on asking yourself what are you not afraid of doing? If you can fail again and again at something and still love it, that's your passion. What are some of the things that you do that failure is never a concern of yours? The enthusiastic mentality consists of people who are consistently doing the things they just love to do without the sense of failing.

Ask yourself: what will you regret not doing?

We all have these dreams, and in our final moments, you will reconcile the things you've wished you did in the past. Even right now, what are some of the things you've wished you did more in the past? If you were dying, what will you regret the most? What will you like to do, but never had a chance to? Think back on the possibilities you've wished you had and the job you've always wanted. Whatever your regrets rely on, this may be a good indicator for where your real passion builds on in. In life, there is nothing worse than having regret, so that's why it's important to pursue your dreams right now. Therefore, finding your passion, and following it is so important. Because you live your life so that you do not have regrets in the future.

These are just a few insightful questions to ask yourself when you want to find out what you are passionate about in life. To sum it all up, passion leads to enthusiasm and knowing what you are passionate about will guarantee your road to a more exciting life.

HOW TO BECOME MORE GRACIOUS?

One of the leading productive ways to build your enthusiasm at your workplace, in business, and in your personal life is always to remind yourself of everything that has been given to you. Express your gratitude for all that have happened, and this will help you become even more excited about what you are doing and the good things that are to come. As we go through the working day, it is very easy to forget all about the things that make our lives simpler and comfortable. Remember all the right things that you have happening in your life and be thankful for the person you are today. This is a realistic and workable way for you to enhance your enthusiasm during the working day.

So here is some practical advice on how any one person can become a deeply grateful compassionate human-being. Here are the things that are required to become a very powerful force of nature and genuinely gracious at all things life has to offer:

Make a commitment to yourself

You need to set a goal for yourself for improvement and commitment to practice becoming a thankful person to the people and things that make up your life. When you wake up in the morning, you should boldly declare to yourself, "I am going to be grateful today."

Gratitude is not a subconscious decision, but you can habitually train your mind to become gracious at everything that you do. Gratitude is a conscious decision. You must practice it consistently for it to soak deep inside your mind. Now for example, if you have a coworker just willing to pick up an item you've dropped, that's a luxury some people don't have, and you should go out of your way to thank them.

Know the value of others around you

We all want to be treated and acknowledge substantially at work, so why not give it to others? To become grateful, you must know the value of others and things in life. For example, it is very easy to forget the value of your coworkers. But they have the same working life as you. You may have already implanted this mindset that "it's their job to be a good worker". However, it's their choice.

If you wish for your life to become more thrilling then pay respect for each small acts of kindness that comes to them, whether it's assistance on their duties, an enlightening compliment, or just being there for them.

Help other people and do good deeds

A practicable approach to gratitude is to practice giving and spreading positivity to the world around you, this can ensure a much better world. Now, many religions and cultures value the fact of helping others and positive energy. By doing these random acts of kindness, it will be repaid to you by a better understanding of the world. Helping others goes a long way. It can make you feel more superior, restore the joys of life, and make people believe that there is hope in humanity.

Goodness pays back equally. Though you should never do something good just because you want to gain something in life. Here are some ideas of how you can give positive energy and help others around your workplace:

1. Pay compliments
2. Ask if you can help your coworkers with anything
3. Volunteer to work overtime
4. Smile more
5. Hold the door for others
6. Write a thank you note for someone whose been working hard
7. Buy a gift for your boss and coworkers
8. Eliminate negativity

It is very easy to be absorbed by our own personal goals and development. But by stepping outside of our daily routines and comfort zones to just help someone, it will provide amazing perspective and insight to fill up your working place with only positive energy.

STOP COMPARING YOURSELF WITH OTHERS

Many people often compare themselves with others, some of us may not even be fully aware that we are comparing ourselves with our coworkers. However, the comparison is only depriving us of the joys of life. With us always saying to ourselves that "Are they better than me." we lower our self-esteem and make us feel bad about ourselves. You must resist the urge to compare boy self with others.

Why would you compare yourself to others, when you are one out of a million? No one else will look like you, think like you, or be you. No one can build themselves up to be exactly like you. Life is about being the bet you possibly can be, not about being the best in the world and certainly not about being someone you are not. Resist the urge to compare yourself, and you will find great gratitude in yourself.

Instead, you should rather compare yourself to...yourself only. Think of "self" as the only "person" you need to compete with. As an example to better grasp the idea, you should not compare your own success to how successful your friends are, but rather ask yourself if you are more successful than you were last year. Making real progress in your life can only be done by not comparing yourself to the many people around you.

REMOVING NEGATIVITY

The only thing that is maybe preventing you from reaching your full potential and level of enthusiasm is negative emotions. If you had no negative emotions at all, and only active ones, will you believe that life is more wondrous and exciting? The person who is enthusiast and happy always have unique perspectives, and they see the world as something meaningful.

Getting rid of negative thinking will be difficult, but not impossible. It's not going to happen overnight; it may take years before you fully embrace your soul. Here is how you can eliminate negative thoughts and emotions that occur in your life.

Letting go of mediocrity and accepting positivity.

For a lot of people, negative emotions seem like a comforting source whenever we face an impossible task. However, we cannot reach happiness if we deliberately approach negativity as the answer to our problems. Thus, it's imperative that we learn to let it go.

The only effective way to release our negative beliefs is that we become conscious and we choose to think a different way. Meaning if you believe that life is only wickedness and is pure despair, you will be living in a wicked and miserable world. But if you feel that life is all fun and games, then there will be more to life than meets the eye. Your thoughts are very powerful if you transfer all your negative thoughts into good ones then it will only manifest itself to the right things in your life.

The less negativity that consists in your life, the less negative you will be in life. Seek out positive people and sources and be bold on the kind of people you allow in your life. Now, with that said. Whenever something bad to you, do your best to see the good side of the situation. If your boss is letting go of employees than think to yourself that it's only because there are, greater opportunities are waiting for you. If your boss is pummeling a huge workload on you, then think of it as your boss only knowing that you can complete it and no one else. Be wary of what enters your mind and soul, only allow the thoughts that create positivity and motivate you to positive actions.

UNDERSTANDING YOURSELF ON A MUCH DEEPER LEVEL

For you to take control in your private life and in at work, you must firstly get to know yourself. Of course, you may believe that it is all easy for one person to identify themselves but I need to ask you something. Who are you? What is your life all about?

Believe me; those are rather difficult questions. But I want you to know that it is important for you to understand who you are and the person that you wish to be. Knowing yourself takes a lifetime. It's all about discovering who you are as a human being and knowing your value to the world. To reach the level of enthusiasm, you must understand who you're fighting for. So, in this chapter, we will be going over how you can know yourself on an earnest level.

Here are a few questions that lead to a real discussion with yourself. Try to answer these questions as honestly as you possibly can. It is also best to write your answers down on paper so you can look at it back on in the future. And as well with that, there are no right or wrong answers. There is only you tapping into your life.

1. What are the things that make you happy?
2. How will you describe yourself?
3. Do you love yourself? Why or why not?
4. What are some things you've learned in life?
5. What is your job and do you love it?
6. What is the most important thing in your life?

7. What are you grateful for?
8. Who are the people you hang out with?
9. What are the things that you love doing, even when you are stressed?
10. What is your greatest fear?
11. Will you help someone in need?
12. What will you tell yourself 5 years in the past?
13. What will you ask yourself 5 years in the future?
14. What do you believe is possible for you?
15. What are your proudest accomplishments?
16. What do you do on your average day?
17. What are your values?
18. How much time are you willing to sacrifice today to guarantee a future?
19. What are you passionate about?
20. What kind of legacy do you want to leave behind?
21. What is your deepest secret?
22. Do you listen to your heart or to your brain?
23. What are you looking for in life?
24. Is it important to love or to give love?
25. Do you care about what others think of you?

26. What do you find funny?

27. What is your top priority right now?

28. What will you do if you have a million dollars?

29. What is love to you?

30. Who is your greatest role model?

31. What is your dream job?

32. What are some things I want to change about?

Now, these questions will surely spark conversation amongst yourself and are imperative to know that you answer the questions as truthfully as you can.

How Can Failures and Setbacks Be a Good Thing?

Part of life is we suffer, we go through failure, and we experience severe setbacks in our life. But what if I can change your perspective about all the negative aspects of life. To achieve great enthusiasm, we must embrace the prospect of failure.

The wisdom you gain from learning from your failures is the only thing you need in life. Failure should not be perceived as an obstacle; it is a necessity that brings you closer to achieving your hopes and dreams. Failing also provides you with a sense of completion and help understand yourself a whole lot more. Just think of it like, how will you handle a failure? Will you give up easily or will you learn from the experience and grow? It's a learning experience. When you fail in one area in your life, you can apply the lessons you've learned from so to make sure that it does not happen again.

Whenever you fail at anything, it is crucial that you learn from it. Finding out the reasons why you've failed in the first place. Do you think that success and happiness will come without failures? No, every enthusiastic person undergoes significant failures, but they were so enthusiastically about the situation that they were proud about their failures.

What are Your Values?

What do you think is the most important thing in your life? Do you value being happy? Do you value financial success? Do you value being in a job you love to wake up to every morning? What exactly do you want in life? What's preventing you from achieving it?

To understand yourself on a deeper note, you must understand your values. Values are the things that you believe are most important in the way you live and the way you work. They determine what you think is important first, and ultimately they shape your life. In many situations at life, understanding what you value can really help you reach your dreams.

STRENGTHENING YOUR WORK ETHIC

If you identify yourself as someone who isn't putting in their all, then you must take the incentive to increase and build up an adamant work ethic to accomplish greater success in your chosen field. Think back to the countless of successful people who have walked on this planet. If you ask them how did they become so successful, I ensure you that the story will always be the same. They've worked harder than the majority, and thus they've achieved such success. It wasn't luck, just sheer hard work. In this section, I will go over what you can do to increase your job ethic.

Realize that nothing worth achieving is easy

If you wish to become more fruitful and enthusiastic every day for the rest of your life, effort must be put. It's not going to be easy. If it was easy, believe me, everybody would've done it. Nothing worth achieving is going to be easy. I need you to understand that working hard and developing a strong work ethic is not going to that fun. It may be painful for some.

But I do need to tell you that those without a strong work ethic will always continue to further themselves from their dreams more and more. It's going to be hard, and it's going to be a struggle, but it is all going to pay off immensely shortly.

If you do not like something, do something about it.

This method is plain simple. If you do not like your job, find a new one. If you don't like your body image, change it. If you don't like your financial situation, do something about it. It's not going to help one bit sitting around being a bum about self-caused circumstances. Your actions and your attitude can change anything in the world. What you think about daily will later manifest itself in the future. So, it is imperative that you think only positive thoughts and that you further yourself away from things you do not like.

Utilize Your Time Effectively

Each person has the same 24 hours in his or her day. Oprah Winfrey, Bill Gates, young, successful, poor, wealthy, and everybody else all have twenty-four hours in a single day. The difference between the enthusiastic and the unenthusiastic is what they do with their time. Those who are enthusiastic about what they do will maximize their time to get the most out of it. Those who are unenthusiastic will use their time recklessly and procrastinate on several factors. If you want to strengthen your work ethic, time and willpower is your answer.

Limit Destructive Activities

As I said before, you must remove yourself from harmful activities and bad thoughts. Many activities in the world can either help you or destroy you. When you are at work, do you text a lot? If so, stop it. When you are working on your business, do you get easily distracted by checking up on Facebook? If so, stop it. If you have activities that are getting you nowhere in life, stop it and replace it with uplifting productive ones.

Surround Yourself with Empowering People

When you do not feel like doing something, it's best to have others who are willing to support and empower you themselves. For example, find and join a support group that stands ready to help you with your problems. Take the incentive to surround yourself with only individuals who want to become more successful and fruitful with everything that they do. Active people and friends will only continue to motivate you to work harder and harder in everything that they do.

Through hard work and with a strong work ethic, you can achieve your dreams and become more enthusiastic in everything that you do.

How to Improve Areas of Your Life

Every year we form New Year's resolutions, it's a way to improve certain areas of your life. It's always great and confident to develop your inner-mind, your body, and your spirit. To become enthusiastic, you should always be consistently working to improve areas in your life.

Here are some of the most crucial areas that you should strive to make improvement in:

Your Health and Fitness

Do you live your life healthily? Do you exercise regularly? Millions and millions of people are always striving for a much better health and body. This can easily be done if you exclude yourself from junk food and develop little exercise routines.

Your Brain

There is always room to expand your mind. The more intellectual you are, the more aware you are. You shed always do your best by always reading on new things. It can be as simple as reading a few articles or through an entire book. You should always be challenging your mind a tad bit more. Brainpower is power!

Your Career

How can you move forward into your career? How can you work even harder? How can you improve certain areas in your life to climb the company's ladder? Well, write down the answer. It will take some time figuring out. But, think big. Don't limit yourself by your standards or other people's standards. We are all capable of accomplishing great things in life.

Your Relationships

AT work, you should improve every relation. As well with that, you should spend loads of time with inspirational people, they will always help you learn different things and give you a fulfilling way to enjoy yourself in life. Ask yourself: what can you do to improve your social life and improve other relations. Once you've done that, go ahead and act.

CONCLUSION

To conclude this entire guidebook, I admit that ideally, I would want you to realize that you can fully declutter your mind once you gain knowledge and perspective. If you've read the book and followed the arguments and perspective, you have made more than the first step. Most of us can walk through our entire life without even knowing what is wrong and why is it so wrong.

My deepest wish for you, my reader, is to make you fully aware of the true possibility that you have to achieve a more thrilling, exciting, and much more interesting life. If the impact is as wanted, sooner rather than later you can become more self-driven and up the energy you have getting up every day.

For you to do so, you must practice and practice and consistently use such techniques daily. I would advise reading through some of the chapters more than once. As you gain perspective, the info and thoughts I gathered in this guidebook will become enriched. Realize that this book was meant to change your life for the better fully, but as it is the case with every act of transmitting a message, through words, it needs your input and open-minded approach.

Now, even if you find it difficult to maintain a high level of enthusiasm, never give up on it. Nobody does it like it's easy. If it were easy, I wouldn't have engaged in writing about it. I would love if you could take me seriously when I state that there are millions and millions of productive, decluttered, successful minds out there and there will continue to be so.

As well with that, if you enjoyed reading this guide or find that this guide holds some value in your life, it will be appreciative if you can kindly leave a positive and upbeat review on here. I wish to reach as many people as I can with this book, and you figure that more honest and authentic reviews will help me accomplish that goal. And once again, thank you very much and the best wishes to you and may your journey be exciting, full of freedom and happiness.

Thank you!

Thank you for downloading this book. I hope you found this book interesting and advices was helpful for you.

Made in the USA
San Bernardino, CA
12 October 2017